CW01558830

DORDOGN...
TRAVEL GUIDE
2025

THELMA JASON

GET ACCESS TO MORE
BOOKS BY THE AUTHOR

TABLE OF CONTENTS

INTRODUCTION: DISCOVERING THE HEART OF DORDOGNE

Nestled in the rolling hills of southwestern France, Dordogne is a region that feels like a step back in time, where every stone, every river, and every forest whispers the stories of centuries past. Known for its enchanting landscapes, Dordogne is a treasure trove of natural beauty, history, and cultural richness. The region, named after the serene Dordogne River that weaves through its heart, stretches across the green plains and rocky outcrops, offering a mix of rugged countryside, fertile valleys, and charming villages.

Dordogne is a place where history isn't confined to the pages of books or the walls of museums; it is alive and woven into the very fabric of the land. The region is home to some of the most significant prehistoric sites in Europe, including the world-famous Lascaux caves. These prehistoric caverns, adorned with ancient artwork that dates back over 17,000 years, offer a rare glimpse into the lives and beliefs of early humans. The cave paintings, depicting animals in vivid detail, speak of a time when the land was inhabited by hunters and gatherers, offering a connection to the distant past that is both humbling and awe-inspiring.

But Dordogne's story does not end there. The region is also known for its remarkable medieval castles, many of which seem to have sprung from the pages of fairy tales. Perched on hilltops and nestled among the valleys, these fortresses and châteaux offer a window into the region's turbulent history, from feudal times to the Hundred Years' War. Each castle is a silent witness to battles, power struggles, and the grandeur of French nobility. Whether exploring the imposing Château de Beynac or the elegant Château de Castelnaud, visitors can almost feel the weight of history in the air, from the stone walls to the panoramic views stretching across the Dordogne valley.

Beyond its historical treasures, Dordogne is a haven for nature lovers. The rolling hills, lush forests, and winding rivers offer countless opportunities for outdoor exploration. The Dordogne River itself is a lifeline, cutting through the landscape and offering a serene route for canoeing or kayaking. Along its banks, ancient towns such as Sarlat-la-Canéda invite visitors to wander through cobbled streets, where time seems to slow down, and every corner holds a story waiting to be uncovered. These towns are filled with exquisite architecture, from medieval stone houses to elegant Renaissance facades, all bathed in the golden light of the region's famous sunsets.

As you travel through Dordogne, you will encounter a region that celebrates its heritage with pride, where local traditions are upheld with passion, and the charm of the past seamlessly blends with the vibrancy of modern life. Here, the pace of life slows, allowing time for reflection, relaxation, and discovery. Whether you're savoring the region's world-class cuisine, exploring its historic sites, or simply enjoying the tranquility of its natural landscapes, Dordogne offers an experience that will leave a lasting impression, making it a must-visit destination for anyone seeking to immerse themselves in the true spirit of France.

Who This Guide is For

This guide is designed for those who seek a deeper connection with the heart and soul of France, offering a unique journey through Dordogne's blend of history, gastronomy, nature, and peaceful charm. Whether you are a history enthusiast, a food lover, a nature seeker, or someone looking for a tranquil yet enriching getaway, Dordogne promises an experience that will captivate your senses and enrich your understanding of this beautiful region.

For history enthusiasts, Dordogne is a treasure trove of ancient wonders. From the awe-inspiring prehistoric cave paintings of Lascaux to the medieval castles that dot the landscape, history comes alive here in a way that is both tangible and immersive. You'll walk in the footsteps of ancient people and explore fortresses once held by knights and royalty, all while uncovering the stories that shaped not just Dordogne, but the entire history of France.

Food lovers will find themselves in culinary heaven in Dordogne. Known as one of the gastronomic capitals of France, the region offers an abundance of fresh, locally sourced ingredients, from truffles and walnuts to foie gras and duck confit. Dordogne's food is simple yet exquisite, with hearty dishes that reflect the land's agricultural abundance and the influence of centuries-old recipes. You'll savor flavors that are rich in tradition, whether you're dining in a charming café, a Michelin-starred restaurant, or a rustic farmhouse kitchen. Each meal here is an opportunity to taste the very essence of the region.

For those who yearn for nature and adventure, Dordogne provides an idyllic setting. The lush, undulating hills, pristine rivers, and dense forests make it a haven for outdoor enthusiasts. Whether you're canoeing along the Dordogne River, hiking through oak-filled woodlands, or cycling through rolling vineyards, the region offers boundless opportunities for exploration. Dordogne's natural beauty is a perfect backdrop for those seeking serenity or outdoor adventures in a peaceful and unspoiled environment.

Lastly, for travelers who are simply looking for a tranquil yet enriching getaway, Dordogne offers an unparalleled sense of peace and timeless charm. Away from the hustle and bustle of everyday life, this region provides an escape into a slower, more deliberate pace of living. You'll find it easy to unwind in the quaint villages, where the scent of fresh-baked bread fills the air and the warm smiles of locals welcome you. Here, relaxation and discovery go hand in hand, making it the perfect destination for anyone looking to recharge while indulging in the region's many offerings.

Whether you are drawn to Dordogne's rich history, its world-class cuisine, its breathtaking landscapes, or its peaceful atmosphere, this guide will help you navigate and fully appreciate the many facets of this incredible region.

Best Times to Visit

Dordogne offers something for every traveler, no matter the time of year, but the best times to visit truly depend on what kind of experience you're seeking.

Spring and Autumn are the sweet spots for anyone wanting to experience Dordogne at its most serene and picturesque. During these seasons, the weather is mild, making it ideal for outdoor activities such as hiking, cycling, or leisurely strolls through the region's charming towns and villages. The spring months, from March to May, bring a burst of vibrant colors, with wildflowers carpeting the meadows and the surrounding hillsides coming to life in a brilliant array of greens. In autumn, from September to November, the landscape shifts into rich shades of amber, gold, and crimson, especially in the vineyards, as the harvest season begins. These shoulder seasons also mean fewer crowds, allowing you to fully enjoy the tranquility and natural beauty of the region without the hustle and bustle of peak tourism. Whether you're exploring prehistoric caves or wandering the cobbled streets of Sarlat, these months offer a perfect balance of mild temperatures and peaceful surroundings.

For those seeking a more festive atmosphere, summer is the season to visit Dordogne. From June to August, the region comes alive with vibrant markets, outdoor concerts, and colorful festivals that celebrate its rich culture and history. The summer months are a perfect time to soak up the lively atmosphere of towns like Bergerac, where the streets buzz with local produce markets, street performances, and bustling cafés. The warmth of summer also brings an ideal opportunity to experience Dordogne's iconic rivers—whether it's kayaking along the Dordogne River, floating down the Vézère, or enjoying riverside picnics by the water. This is also the time when the region's food festivals come to life, including those dedicated to truffles, foie gras, and local wines. If you love the buzz of a lively local culture, summer is the best time to visit, with its festive markets and cultural events adding an extra layer of excitement to your experience.

However, it's important to note that the peak summer months can bring slightly higher temperatures and more tourists, especially around the most popular attractions like the Lascaux caves or the medieval town of Sarlat. If you prefer to enjoy the best of both worlds—mild weather, fewer tourists, and vibrant landscapes—then the spring and autumn months are undoubtedly the ideal time to visit Dordogne.

No matter the season, Dordogne's beauty and charm are ever-present, ensuring that each visit promises a unique and memorable experience.

CHAPTER 1: ESSENTIAL TRAVEL TIPS

Before setting off to explore Dordogne, it's important to prepare in order to fully appreciate everything the region has to offer. Here are a few key travel tips to ensure a smooth and memorable experience:

Currency & Payments

The official currency in Dordogne, as in the rest of France, is the Euro (€). While credit cards are widely accepted in larger towns, cities, and tourist areas, it's always a good idea to carry cash for smaller villages, rural areas, or local markets where cash is often the preferred method of payment. Some family-run cafés, artisanal shops, and local markets may not accept credit cards, or there may be a minimum purchase required for card transactions.

ATMs are readily available in major towns like Sarlat-la-Canéda, Périgueux, and Bergerac, allowing you to easily withdraw cash if needed. Be sure to inform your bank of your travel dates to avoid any issues with your credit or debit cards while abroad.

Additionally, while the contactless payment system is becoming more popular, it's still a good idea to have a small amount of cash on hand for small purchases such as pastries from a boulangerie, local souvenirs, or tips for service staff. In some of the more rural areas, the local markets or guesthouses might only accept cash, so planning accordingly will save you time and ensure you're never caught without payment options.

For international visitors, it's worth noting that foreign credit cards (especially those that don't have a chip) might face limitations in smaller shops or older card machines. To avoid any inconvenience, use cards with a chip-and-PIN feature, or better yet, a contactless card for faster payments.

In terms of tipping, while service charges are typically included in the bill (indicated by "service compris") in restaurants, it's common to leave small tips for excellent service. Rounding up the bill in cafés, bars, or for taxi rides is also appreciated but not required. A small tip of 1-2 euros for baristas, hotel staff, or taxi drivers is a nice gesture to show appreciation for good service.

Time Zone

Dordogne, like the rest of France, follows Central European Time (CET) during the standard time period, which is UTC+1. However, during daylight saving time (from the last Sunday in March to the last Sunday in October), the region observes Central European Summer Time (CEST), shifting the time to UTC+2.

This means that if you're traveling from outside of Europe, it's important to account for the time difference, which can vary depending on where you're coming from. For example, New York is 6 hours behind CET and 7 hours behind during CEST, while London is 1 hour behind year-round.

Be mindful of the time change when planning activities or catching transport, as some schedules (especially for trains and flights) may shift slightly with the seasons. Also, this time shift means you'll have longer daylight hours during the summer months, making it ideal for sightseeing, outdoor activities, and enjoying Dordogne's picturesque landscapes.

Packing Checklist

When packing for Dordogne, comfort and practicality are key, as the region is known for its beautiful yet sometimes rugged landscapes, with plenty of outdoor exploration, ancient sites, and charming villages to visit. Here's a checklist to ensure you have everything you need for an unforgettable experience.

• **Comfortable Walking Shoes:** Dordogne is a region best explored on foot, from wandering through medieval villages to hiking along scenic trails or touring castles and caves. Pack sturdy, comfortable walking shoes that can handle uneven surfaces and the occasional steep incline. Opt for shoes with good support, as you'll likely spend much of your time on your feet.

• **Lightweight, Breathable Clothing:** If visiting in the warmer months (spring to early autumn), lightweight, breathable clothing is essential to keep you comfortable. Cotton or moisture-wicking fabrics will keep you cool during day-long explorations. Pack layers, as mornings and evenings can be cooler, especially in rural areas or in the caves.

• **Sunscreen and Hat:** The Dordogne region boasts lots of sunshine, especially in the summer. Protect yourself from the sun by packing sunscreen with a high SPF and a wide-brimmed hat to keep cool while you explore.

• **Water Bottle:** Staying hydrated is essential, especially when visiting outdoor sites like the caves, castles, and vineyards. Carry a reusable water bottle that you can refill throughout the day to stay refreshed.

• **Camera or Smartphone:** Dordogne is a photographer's paradise, with its rolling hills, historic sites, and idyllic countryside. Don't forget a camera or your smartphone to capture all the stunning vistas and memories.

• **Swimwear:** If you're planning to take a dip in one of Dordogne's beautiful rivers, lakes, or pools, don't forget your swimwear. The summer months provide plenty of opportunities for a refreshing swim.

- **Bug Repellent:** Depending on the time of year, insects, especially mosquitoes, can be a nuisance, particularly near rivers and lakes. A good insect repellent is a must to avoid bites, especially in the evenings.

- **Travel Adapters:** If traveling from outside Europe, be sure to bring a travel adapter for your electronics, as France uses Type C and E plugs with a voltage of 230V and frequency of 50Hz.

- **Small Backpack:** For day trips, a small, lightweight backpack is ideal for carrying essentials like water, snacks, a camera, and a light jacket.

- **Cash and Cards:** While credit cards are widely accepted in tourist areas, some smaller villages, markets, and local shops may only accept cash. Be sure to carry some Euros, particularly if you're planning to explore off the beaten path.

With this checklist in hand, you'll be well-prepared to enjoy Dordogne's stunning natural beauty, fascinating history, and charming villages to the fullest.

- **Swimsuit for River Activities or Visiting Outdoor Pools:** Dordogne is known for its beautiful rivers, offering plenty of opportunities for swimming, kayaking, or simply relaxing by the water. Be sure to pack a swimsuit if you're planning to take a dip in the Dordogne River or any of the region's outdoor pools, especially during the warmer months when the weather is ideal for water activities.

• **Portable Charger for Long Excursions in Remote Areas:** While exploring Dordogne's picturesque villages, castles, and caves, you might find yourself in areas with limited access to power outlets. A portable charger is a great way to ensure your phone, camera, or other devices stay charged during long excursions, especially if you're using them for navigation or capturing photos of the region's scenic landscapes.

• **A Small Bag for Local Markets and Souvenirs:** Dordogne is home to vibrant local markets, where you can find everything from handmade goods to fresh produce and local delicacies. A small, lightweight bag is perfect for carrying your purchases, whether you're picking up a bottle of local wine, some cheese, or unique souvenirs to remember your trip by. A crossbody or foldable bag is especially useful for convenience and comfort while strolling through market stalls.

With these additional items, you'll be well-prepared to embrace all that Dordogne has to offer, from leisurely river activities to exploring local markets and capturing lasting memories from your journey.

Health & Safety:

• Emergency Numbers: In Dordogne, as in the rest of France, it's essential to know the emergency numbers in case of an unexpected situation.

• **Police (Police Secours): 17**

- **Ambulance (SAMU - Service d'Aide Médicale Urgente): 15**

- **Fire Department (Pompiers): 18**

- **European Emergency Number (General Emergency):** 112 (works across the EU for all emergency services)

These numbers will connect you directly to the appropriate services in case of any emergencies. Be sure to keep these numbers saved on your phone and know their locations relative to where you'll be staying in case you need to act quickly.

Additionally, it's wise to familiarize yourself with the nearest hospital or clinic to your accommodation before heading to Dordogne. Many areas have local medical centers that can assist with minor issues, while larger towns like Périgueux and Bergerac offer hospitals and medical facilities for more significant concerns.

Before your trip, ensure that you have adequate travel insurance that covers health emergencies, especially if you plan on engaging in more physically demanding activities, such as hiking, cycling, or swimming in natural water sources.

Health Insurance Tips for EU and Non-EU Travelers:

- **For EU Travelers:** If you're traveling from within the European Union, ensure that you have a valid

European Health Insurance Card (EHIC) or its replacement, the GHIC (Global Health Insurance Card) for UK residents. This card grants you access to necessary state-provided healthcare services during your stay in France, often at reduced costs or free of charge, depending on the nature of the treatment. However, the EHIC does not cover private healthcare, so you may still want to have additional travel insurance to cover any unforeseen circumstances, such as accidents or trip cancellations.

• **For Non-EU Travelers:** If you're coming from outside the EU, travel health insurance is highly recommended, and in some cases, it may be required. Check with your insurance provider to ensure that you're covered for emergency medical treatment, hospital stays, and any activities that might be more physically demanding (e.g., hiking, cycling, or swimming in natural bodies of water). Make sure your plan also covers medical evacuation in case you need to be transported back home for treatment.

Before purchasing travel insurance, double-check that it includes coverage for the entire duration of your stay, including any adventurous activities you may plan to engage in during your trip to Dordogne.

Travel Vaccinations (If Any) to Check Before Visiting:

France, including Dordogne, does not have any specific vaccination requirements for travelers unless you're coming from a region where certain diseases are prevalent (e.g., yellow fever). However, it is recommended to ensure you are up-to-date with the following basic vaccinations before traveling to France:

1. **Routine vaccinations:** Make sure your routine vaccinations are up to date, including those for measles, mumps, rubella (MMR), diphtheria, tetanus, and pertussis, polio, and influenza (especially during winter months).

2. **Hepatitis A:** This is generally recommended if you're visiting rural areas, as it can be contracted through contaminated food or water, though the risk is low in tourist areas.

3. **Hepatitis B:** If you plan on engaging in activities like unprotected sex or using needles (e.g., in medical settings), this vaccination might be advisable.

4. **Tick-borne encephalitis:** If you're planning to explore Dordogne's forests or engage in outdoor activities in rural areas, consider getting vaccinated against tick-borne encephalitis, a virus transmitted by ticks found in woodland areas.

5. **Rabies:** Rabies vaccinations are recommended only if you plan to have close contact with animals, especially in more remote rural areas. However, the risk is generally low for tourists.

It's always best to consult with your healthcare provider or a travel health clinic several weeks before your trip to ensure you're fully protected, particularly if you're traveling from outside the EU or will be engaging in high-risk activities.

Outdoor Safety Precautions for Hiking or Canoeing in Dordogne

1. Hiking Safety:

- **Choose the Right Trail:** Dordogne offers a variety of hiking trails, ranging from easy village walks to more challenging forest paths and hill hikes. Always research the trail's difficulty level before setting out. Make sure you're aware of the estimated duration and terrain of your chosen route.

- **Wear Proper Footwear:** Sturdy, comfortable hiking boots are essential, especially on rocky or uneven terrain. Waterproof shoes are advisable for hikes near rivers or damp areas, where trails may be slippery.

• **Stay on Marked Trails:** Stick to designated hiking trails to avoid getting lost or straying into private property. Maps, trail markers, and local guidebooks can help you navigate the best paths.

• **Carry Plenty of Water:** The weather in Dordogne can be warm, especially in summer. Make sure you carry enough water to stay hydrated, particularly on longer hikes where facilities may be scarce. A hydration pack or bottle is a good option.

• **Dress in Layers:** Weather can change quickly, especially in the forests or higher altitudes. Wear layers so you can adjust your clothing as needed. Bring a light rain jacket, even on clear days, in case of sudden showers.

• **Inform Someone of Your Plans:** If you're planning on hiking in more remote areas, it's a good idea to tell someone your route and expected return time. In case of an emergency, this could be helpful for rescuers.

• **Know the Signs of Heat Exhaustion:** If you're hiking in summer, keep an eye on yourself and fellow hikers for signs of heat exhaustion, such as dizziness, excessive sweating, or nausea. Rest frequently in shaded areas and drink plenty of water.

• **Pack a First Aid Kit:** Even for short hikes, it's important to have basic first aid supplies with you, such as bandages, antiseptic wipes, blister pads, and pain relievers. If you're in a more remote area, consider packing a map, compass, or GPS device to ensure you can find your way if needed.

2. Canoeing Safety:

• **Wear a Life Jacket:** No matter how confident you are in your swimming ability, always wear a life jacket when canoeing. Even experienced paddlers can find themselves in trouble if they capsize or encounter rough water unexpectedly.

• **Check the Weather:** Before setting out on a canoe trip along the Dordogne River, check the weather forecast. Sudden rainstorms or winds can create dangerous conditions. Avoid going out if heavy rains are expected, as water levels can rise quickly.

• **Know the River's Conditions:** The Dordogne River can vary in speed and difficulty depending on the section. Some areas are calm and ideal for beginners, while others, especially near rapids, may be more suitable for experienced paddlers. Make sure to choose a section of the river that matches your skill level.

• **Wear Sun Protection:** Canoeing exposes you to direct sunlight for long periods, so apply sunscreen regularly and wear protective clothing such as a hat and sunglasses. Reapply sunscreen throughout the day to avoid sunburn.

• **Bring a Dry Bag:** Keep your valuables dry by using a waterproof dry bag for your phone, wallet, and other essentials. In case of a spill or unexpected weather, having dry clothing and supplies will make your experience much more comfortable.

• **Be Aware of Water Hazards:** Keep an eye out for submerged rocks, fallen trees, or fast-moving currents that could cause capsizing or accidents. Stay alert and avoid risky maneuvers, especially near unfamiliar parts of the river.

• **Paddle in Pairs:** If you're new to canoeing, it's often a good idea to go out with someone who has more experience. Paddling with a partner helps ensure better stability and can be crucial in case of emergencies.

• **Respect River Traffic:** The Dordogne River can be busy with other canoes, kayaks, and boats, especially near towns. Be courteous to other river-goers, and always follow local rules or guidelines.

• **Plan Your Route and Timing:** If you plan on paddling a long stretch of the river, consider how long it will take and plan your trip around daylight hours. Bring a map or GPS device so you can stay on track, and make sure you know where you will be able to exit the river.

By following these outdoor safety precautions, whether you're hiking or canoeing in Dordogne, you'll be able to fully enjoy your adventures while staying safe and prepared for any unexpected situations.

CHAPTER 2: TRANSPORTATION AND GETTING AROUND IN DORDOGNE

How to Get There:

By Air:

When planning your trip to Dordogne, one of the most common methods of arrival is by air, and there are two primary airports you should consider based on your departure city and travel preferences: Bergerac Dordogne Périgord Airport and Bordeaux-Mérignac Airport. Each serves different travel needs, whether you're seeking the convenience of a budget-friendly flight or the comfort of international connections.

Bergerac Dordogne Périgord Airport (EGC)

Bergerac Airport is an excellent choice if you're arriving from within Europe, particularly from the UK or other major European cities. It's a small yet well-connected airport located just 15 to 20 kilometers from the Dordogne region's key towns and villages, making it the most convenient option for those wishing to minimize their travel time once they arrive in France.

• **Low-Cost Flights:** Bergerac is served by several budget airlines, including Ryanair and EasyJet, offering direct routes from major cities like London, Dublin, Brussels, and more. This makes it an affordable option for many travelers looking to explore Dordogne on a budget. Whether you're traveling for a long weekend or an extended stay, you'll find frequent flights that often provide great deals, especially if you book well in advance.

• **Airport Facilities:** Although Bergerac is a smaller regional airport, it offers all the essential services travelers need, including car rental counters, tourist information, baggage handling, and small cafes. The airport may not have the extensive facilities of a major international airport, but it's streamlined and efficient for travelers on the go.

• **Transportation from Bergerac Airport:** Once you land, getting from the airport to the heart of Dordogne is straightforward. Car hire is the most popular option, as it gives you the flexibility to explore the region at your own pace. Car rental agencies such as Hertz, Avis, and Europcar are available at the airport, with most major brands offering competitive pricing. You can also take a taxi or private shuttle, but renting a car will likely be your most convenient and cost-effective option, especially if you plan to visit multiple towns and attractions scattered across the region.

• **Travel Time:** The drive from Bergerac Airport to popular Dordogne destinations like Sarlat-la-Canéda takes about 40 minutes, while reaching the wine-producing region of Bergerac is just 25 minutes away. This makes the airport a very accessible entry point for anyone staying in or around Dordogne.

Bordeaux-Mérignac Airport (BOD)

For travelers coming from beyond Europe or those seeking more international flight options, Bordeaux-Mérignac Airport is the gateway to Dordogne. Located about two hours west of the Dordogne region, Bordeaux-Mérignac is a larger international airport offering a wider variety of flights, making it an ideal choice for visitors who don't mind a longer transfer time.

• **International Flights:** Bordeaux-Mérignac is the main international hub for the southwestern part of France. Major airlines such as Air France, British Airways, and KLM provide regular services to and from global cities such as New York, London, Amsterdam, and Paris, among others. It's a great option if you're flying from outside Europe or need a wider range of flight options.

• **Airport Facilities:** As a larger airport, Bordeaux-Mérignac offers a wider range of services, including more shops, restaurants, duty-free options, and additional facilities like lounges and free Wi-Fi. There's also an information desk to help guide you on how to reach Dordogne, as well as places to purchase regional products like wine and gourmet foods. For those arriving on international flights, you'll find a smoother transition with customs and baggage handling.

• **Transportation from Bordeaux Airport:** The airport is well-connected to the Dordogne region, but since it's farther than Bergerac, the journey will require more planning. The most common transportation options include:

• **Car rental:** Rent a car at Bordeaux-Mérignac to give you ultimate flexibility while traveling in the Dordogne. The drive from Bordeaux to Sarlat, one of the most famous Dordogne towns, takes approximately 2 hours via the A89 highway. Renting a car gives you the freedom to stop at charming villages along the way, such as Bergerac or Lascaux, without relying on public transport.

• **Train:** You can take a train from Bordeaux to various parts of Dordogne, particularly Perigueux or Bergerac. Trains from Bordeaux are relatively frequent, with journeys to Bergerac taking about 2 hours. For Sarlat, you'll need to change at Les Eyzies or Perigueux, and the entire trip can take around 2.5 to 3 hours. Though it's slower than driving, taking the train allows you to sit back and enjoy the scenic countryside.

- **Bus and Shuttle Services:** If you're traveling on a budget, there are also buses and shuttle services from Bordeaux to the Dordogne region. The journey can take 3 to 4 hours, depending on traffic and your destination.

- **Travel Time:** Bordeaux's airport is about 2 hours away from Dordogne's prime attractions, like Sarlat and La Roque-Gageac. Even though the distance is longer, the more frequent international flights may make Bordeaux a more attractive option, especially for those traveling from overseas.

Other Ways to Access Dordogne

While flying into one of these airports is the most common route, Dordogne is also reachable via train or bus from other major French cities like Paris and Toulouse. High-speed trains, including the TGV, connect Bordeaux to Paris in under 3 hours, and from Bordeaux, you can transfer to regional trains that will take you deeper into Dordogne.

However, keep in mind that public transportation is less frequent in rural Dordogne, and once you arrive in the region, renting a car will be the best way to get around. The picturesque nature of Dordogne's small villages, castles, and countryside makes driving an enjoyable and convenient way to explore.

Final Thoughts on Air Travel to Dordogne

Choosing the right airport for your arrival in Dordogne depends on your travel priorities—whether it's the budget-friendly convenience of Bergerac or the wide-reaching options of Bordeaux. Both airports offer seamless connections to Dordogne, allowing you to dive straight into the beauty of this stunning region, whether by car, train, or shuttle. By understanding these options, you can better plan your travel and optimize your time in this charming part of southwestern France.

By Train

The SNCF (Société Nationale des Chemins de fer Français) train network offers an exceptional and scenic way to travel to and within Dordogne. If you're looking for an immersive travel experience, there's no better way to explore the French countryside than by train. This mode of transport allows you to relax, take in the views, and avoid the hassle of driving.

Getting to Dordogne from Major Cities:

• **From Paris:** The high-speed TGV (Train à Grande Vitesse) connects Paris to Bordeaux in just over 2 hours, and from Bordeaux, you can easily transfer to regional trains heading deeper into Dordogne. The journey from Paris to Périgueux (the capital of Dordogne) takes around 4 to 5 hours, while Sarlat-la-Canéda, one of the region's most famous towns, can be reached in approximately 5 hours. The Paris-Bordeaux leg is particularly scenic as you move through the lush, green regions of the Loire and Aquitaine before reaching the Dordogne.

• **From Bordeaux:** Bordeaux is a major transportation hub for the region and a great starting point for train journeys to Dordogne. The trip from Bordeaux to Bergerac takes approximately 1 hour, and the journey to Périgueux takes about 2 hours. Regional trains from Bordeaux are regular, comfortable, and offer great views of the rural landscapes as you head east toward Dordogne. If you're staying in the town of Sarlat, you'll need to make a transfer at Les Eyzies or Périgueux, and the total travel time can range between 2.5 to 3 hours.

• **Other Connections:** The SNCF network also connects Dordogne to other cities in France, such as Toulouse and Limoges. Travelers from these locations will find the train journey to Dordogne relaxing, and the region's rural beauty becomes more pronounced as you approach.

Why Take the Train to Dordogne?

• Scenic Journeys: One of the best aspects of taking the train to Dordogne is the stunning scenery that unfolds along the way. Whether you're traveling from Paris, Bordeaux, or another French city, the train provides panoramic views of vineyards, châteaux, and the iconic river valleys that define Dordogne's landscape. The journey is a prelude to the tranquil beauty you'll find upon arrival, making the train ride part of the experience.

•	**Comfort and Convenience:** Trains in France are comfortable and well-equipped, offering spacious seating, air-conditioning, and onboard services such as cafés or snack bars. The French rail network is known for its punctuality, making it a reliable choice for travelers. Unlike flights, there's no need to arrive hours early at the station—typically, arriving 30 minutes before departure is enough. The stations are well-signposted and have facilities to accommodate tourists, including luggage storage and helpful tourist information.

•	**Eco-Friendly Travel:** For those concerned with their environmental footprint, traveling by train is an eco-friendly alternative to flying or driving. The French rail network operates on electricity, much of which comes from renewable sources, making it one of the greenest ways to explore the country.

•	**No Parking Hassles:** Traveling by train also eliminates the stress of finding parking in Dordogne's small villages and towns, especially in more popular spots like Sarlat or La Roque-Gageac, where parking can be limited and difficult to navigate.

Train Stations in Dordogne:

Once you arrive in Dordogne, the region has several key train stations that serve as gateways to the surrounding villages and attractions.

• **Bergerac Station (Gare de Bergerac):** This station is one of the main entry points to Dordogne. Located just a short distance from the town center, it offers connections to Bordeaux and beyond. From Bergerac, you can easily rent a car, take a taxi, or use local transport to explore nearby villages.

• **Périgueux Station (Gare de Périgueux):** Périgueux is the capital of Dordogne and an important train hub for the region. It has direct connections to Bordeaux and Paris, with options for regional connections to other towns in the area. The station is conveniently located near the town center, so once you arrive, you're just a short walk from the charming streets of Périgueux.

• **Sarlat Station (Gare de Sarlat-la-Canéda):** Sarlat is one of the most popular tourist destinations in Dordogne, though it doesn't have a major train station in the town itself. Instead, you'll need to take a train to Les Eyzies or Périgueux and then transfer to a bus or local transport to reach Sarlat. This extra step makes Sarlat a little less accessible by train compared to other Dordogne destinations, but the charming medieval town is well worth the effort.

Practical Tips for Train Travel in Dordogne:

• **Booking Tickets:** You can purchase train tickets for both TGV and regional services online through the official SNCF website or app, or at ticket machines or counters at train stations. It's advisable to book in advance, especially for TGV services, as these trains can fill up quickly during peak travel times like summer or holiday weekends. Regional train tickets are more flexible and can be bought on the day of travel.

- **Seat Reservations:** While high-speed TGV trains require reservations, most regional trains in Dordogne do not. However, if you're traveling during a busy season, reserving your seat in advance can provide peace of mind. If you're traveling with a rail pass, be sure to check whether seat reservations are included.

- **Schedules:** Train schedules in Dordogne are generally consistent, but they may vary by season. In high tourist seasons, trains may be more frequent, but it's always a good idea to double-check schedules, especially if you're traveling in the off-season. French train stations are well-organized, and information is typically provided in both French and English.

Final Thoughts on Train Travel to Dordogne:

Taking the train to Dordogne is not only a practical and relaxing option but also an enjoyable way to begin your journey into one of France's most picturesque regions. With scenic routes, comfortable services, and convenient connections, the train allows you to sit back and appreciate the landscapes before you even reach your destination. Whether you're arriving from Paris, Bordeaux, or elsewhere in France, taking the train is a great way to start your adventure in Dordogne with minimal stress and maximum enjoyment.

By Car

Renting a car is perhaps the most convenient and recommended option for traveling through Dordogne, especially for those wishing to explore the region's many picturesque villages, hidden gems, and scenic landscapes at their own pace. While public transportation and trains serve the larger towns, many of Dordogne's most captivating attractions are tucked away in the countryside, making a car the ideal choice for those who want the flexibility to venture off the beaten path.

Why Renting a Car is Essential:

• **Access to Remote Villages and Hidden Gems:** Dordogne is a region filled with charming villages and historical sites that are often not easily accessible by public transport. Places like Domme, perched on a hilltop with sweeping views of the Dordogne River, La Roque-Gageac, a village clinging to the cliffside, and Saint-Amand-de-Coly, with its stunning medieval abbey, are often best reached by car. Without a vehicle, you may miss these picturesque locations, which offer the true essence of Dordogne's timeless beauty.

•   **Flexibility and Freedom:** Renting a car gives you the freedom to travel at your own pace. You can start your day early, explore multiple towns in one go, or linger longer at any destination that catches your eye. The absence of rigid schedules allows you to enjoy the region's slower pace of life, stopping for impromptu photos of the rolling countryside, medieval châteaux, or idyllic vineyards. It also makes it easy to visit rural markets or enjoy leisurely meals in out-of-the-way eateries that may not be as accessible by public transport.

•   **Scenic Drives:** Dordogne is home to some of the most beautiful driving routes in France. From the Dordogne Valley to the Vézère Valley, you'll pass through winding roads that offer panoramic views of rivers, forests, and hillside villages. Driving through the region, especially during the golden hours of sunrise and sunset, provides the perfect backdrop for unforgettable experiences. The roads themselves are part of the adventure, as they take you past stone cottages, grapevines, and breathtaking natural landscapes.

How to Rent a Car:

Renting a car in Dordogne is easy, and you have several options to choose from:

• **Airports and Major Train Stations:** If you're flying into Bergerac, Bordeaux, or Limoges, you'll find several international car rental agencies available at these airports. Rental agencies at airports offer a wide range of vehicles, from compact cars to larger SUVs. Similarly, larger train stations like Périgueux and Bordeaux also have car rental options. However, booking in advance is recommended, especially during peak seasons (spring, summer, and holidays).

• **Local Car Rental Companies:** If you're already in the region and need a car, you can rent from local companies in towns like Sarlat, Bergerac, or Périgueux. These smaller agencies are often more flexible and may offer more personalized service than larger chains. Prices can be slightly more competitive, but availability may be limited in high-demand periods, so booking in advance is still advisable.

• **Car Rental Costs:** Prices for renting a car in Dordogne vary based on the time of year, type of car, and rental duration. In general, expect to pay around €30-€60 per day for a small car in low season, with prices rising in the peak summer months. Additional fees, such as insurance, GPS, or extra driver charges, may apply. When booking, compare prices from different rental agencies and check the terms for fuel, mileage, and drop-off charges. It's a good idea to book early for better rates, especially if you plan to visit in high season.

• **Driving License and Insurance:** You will need a valid driving license to rent a car in France. For non-EU travelers, an International Driving Permit (IDP) may be required, so check the regulations for your specific country before booking. In terms of insurance, most car rental agencies provide basic coverage, but it's worth considering additional coverage (like collision damage waiver) for peace of mind. You may also want to consider superior insurance if you plan on driving in more remote or narrow areas, where the risk of minor scratches and dents can be higher.

Driving in Dordogne:

• **Road Conditions and Layout:** The roads in Dordogne are generally in good condition, but they can be narrow, winding, and sometimes unpaved, especially in rural areas. Expect to drive through small, charming lanes, often bordered by hedgerows or stone walls, and be prepared for some hilly terrain. While the main roads are well-marked, secondary routes can sometimes be less straightforward. Use a reliable GPS or map app to avoid getting lost.

• **Parking in Towns and Villages:** In towns like Sarlat, Périgueux, and Bergerac, parking can be a bit challenging during peak hours or tourist season. However, there are usually designated parking lots on the outskirts of the town centers, and free parking options are available in many smaller villages. In some of the medieval towns, like Domme, parking is limited near the old town, so you may need to park a little outside and walk into the heart of the village. Be mindful of any restricted areas, especially in town centers where cars may not be allowed.

• **Speed Limits and Road Signs:** Speed limits in rural areas are generally set at 90 km/h (56 mph) on open roads, and 50 km/h (31 mph) in towns. Watch out for road signs indicating changes in speed limits, as they can be stricter in villages or near historical landmarks. Always obey traffic signals, especially in smaller villages, where pedestrians and cyclists share the roads.

• **Toll Roads:** There are no tolls on most of Dordogne's roads. However, if you're driving from Paris or Bordeaux, you might encounter toll roads on your way to the region, particularly along the A10. These tolls are typically between €10-€25 depending on your route. Be prepared with cash or credit cards, as these tolls are frequently automated, and you'll need to pay at booths along the highway.

Navigating Dordogne's Villages:

Many of Dordogne's towns and villages have medieval layouts, which can make driving through the center challenging. While streets may be quaint and picturesque, they can also be narrow and winding. When driving in these old towns, be prepared for:

• **One-Way Streets:** Many historical centers have one-way streets to control traffic flow, especially in popular towns like Sarlat. Be sure to follow signs carefully and look out for pedestrian zones, where cars are prohibited.

• **Pedestrian Traffic:** In towns like Sarlat and Bergerac, which are popular with tourists, expect to encounter pedestrians, particularly in the old town areas.

Keep an eye out for local markets, which often take place on weekends, and be prepared for temporary roadblocks or detours.

Final Thoughts on Renting a Car in Dordogne:

Renting a car in Dordogne provides unparalleled access to one of France's most beautiful and diverse regions. Whether you're driving through vineyard-laden hills, stopping at quiet villages for a bite of local fare, or heading to remote prehistoric sites like Lascaux, a car ensures that you get the most out of your Dordogne experience. With its scenic routes, charming roads, and access to some of the region's most stunning spots, driving offers the flexibility, freedom, and convenience that no other mode of transport can match.

CHAPTER 3: GETTING AROUND THE REGION

Navigating Dordogne by car is not only convenient but often essential for fully experiencing all that this enchanting region has to offer. While the well-maintained roads connect the larger towns and cities, much of the beauty and charm of Dordogne lies in its rural landscapes, hilltop villages, and off-the-beaten-path attractions that can only be accessed via smaller, winding roads.

The Joy of Exploring by Car:

A car gives you the freedom to travel beyond the well-known spots, venturing into the tranquil countryside, where you'll discover medieval villages, ancient caves, vineyards, and serene riversides that are quintessential to

Dordogne's identity. Without a car, it can be challenging to reach the region's more remote gems, such as the stunning Caves of Lascaux, the medieval fortress town of Beynac-et-Cazenac, or the peaceful hamlets tucked away in the Dordogne Valley.

Roads in Dordogne:

The region's road network is made up of both main highways and narrow, winding lanes. The main routes connecting major towns like Bergerac, Périgueux, Sarlat, and Domme are generally in good condition and easy to navigate. However, as you venture deeper into the countryside, you'll encounter smaller, less-traveled roads that can be a bit more challenging, but also where the magic of Dordogne truly lies.

Main Roads vs. Rural Routes:

•   Main Roads: Dordogne's main roads, especially those connecting larger towns, are well-maintained, often wide enough for two vehicles to pass. These are typically signposted clearly and connect key points of interest, so if you're traveling between towns like Sarlat and Bergerac, or exploring the famous Dordogne Valley, you'll find driving straightforward and efficient.

•   **Rural Roads:** As you head off into the countryside to visit the smaller villages or nature spots, the roads become more narrow, sometimes winding through dense forests or criss crossing river valleys. Some of these rural routes may not be as well-lit at night or may have steep inclines. When traveling on these roads, it's important to drive slowly and be prepared for sudden curves, especially when crossing through forests or vineyards where visibility can be limited.

Narrow Roads and Tight Corners:

In the hilltop villages like Domme and Saint-Amand-de-Coly, the streets are often narrow, stone-paved, and lined with houses that date back to the medieval era. Here, driving can be a bit tricky, especially if you're not used to tight corners or steep inclines. In some of these older villages, you may need to navigate one-way streets or pedestrian zones during busier times, which can add to the challenge. It's advisable to park outside these centers and explore on foot if you don't feel comfortable driving through the narrow lanes.

Toll Roads:

While the majority of Dordogne's roads are free to use, if you're coming from Bordeaux or Paris, you may find yourself on toll roads (especially the A10 highway). These routes are more direct and allow you to bypass smaller towns, but they require a toll fee. Tolls usually range from €10 to €20, depending on the distance traveled. You can pay at the toll booths using cash or credit cards, and having some coins on hand can make the process quicker.

Safety Tips for Driving in Dordogne:

•   **Stay Alert on Narrow Roads:** Some of the smaller roads can be quite narrow and have no shoulder, so be extra cautious when driving through areas with little to no road markings. Always yield to oncoming vehicles when necessary, as there might not be enough space for two cars to pass in some sections.

•   **Watch for Cyclists:** Cycling is a popular activity in Dordogne, especially along the Loire à Vélo route, which spans the region. Be mindful of cyclists on the road, particularly on rural routes. Slower speeds and patience are key in these areas, as cyclists may not always be visible around corners.

•   **Take Care When Driving in the Dark:** While most roads are adequately lit at night, the more rural areas and smaller villages can be quite dark after sunset. It's best to avoid traveling on narrow country lanes at night, particularly if you're unfamiliar with the roads. Stick to main routes, where signage and lighting are better.

•   **Speed Limits:** Speed limits in Dordogne are generally 50 km/h (31 mph) in villages and towns, and 80-90 km/h (50-56 mph) on rural roads. Always check for speed limit signs, especially in towns where the limits may change frequently. When driving in more rural or forested areas, reduce your speed, as wildlife crossing the roads is common, especially at dusk and dawn.

Where to Park:

Parking is generally easy to find in larger towns like Bergerac and Sarlat, where there are designated parking lots. However, in smaller, medieval villages like Beynac, La Roque-Gageac, and Domme, parking can be more challenging, especially during the high tourist season. These villages often have limited parking spaces, so it's a good idea to park in designated lots outside the town center and walk in. Many towns have free parking near tourist attractions, though some, like Sarlat, may charge a small fee.

In more remote areas, you'll likely find free parking near popular walking trails or nature spots, though be sure to check parking signs to avoid fines.

Advantages of Driving Through Dordogne:

• **Freedom to Explore:** Renting a car allows you to explore at your own pace without the restrictions of timetables or routes. You can visit historical sites, take spontaneous detours, and discover hidden gems that most tourists miss.

• **Stunning Scenic Routes:** Dordogne is home to some of the most breathtaking landscapes in France, and driving through its rolling hills, dense forests, and meandering rivers offers some of the best views. The roads themselves are part of the journey—winding past vineyards, orchards, and clifftop villages that seem almost frozen in time.

• **Access to Authentic Experiences:** While Dordogne's towns like Sarlat and Périgueux are famous, some of the region's most memorable experiences can be found in less-visited spots. A car allows you to visit remote caves, prehistoric sites, and quaint villages where you can enjoy local delicacies or shop at farmers' markets without the crowds.

Conclusion:

Driving in Dordogne is the best way to immerse yourself in the region's natural beauty, rich history, and quiet charm. Whether you're exploring its medieval villages, meandering through its vineyard-covered hills, or visiting prehistoric caves, a car provides the ultimate flexibility and convenience. While the winding, narrow roads might take a bit of getting used to, they offer a route to the heart of Dordogne's captivating landscapes and timeless character. So buckle up, embrace the freedom of the open road, and let Dordogne reveal itself to you one picturesque turn at a time.

Public Transport:

In Dordogne, while public transport is available, it is important to know that options can be limited in the more rural areas. The region is known for its beautiful countryside, and much of its charm lies in its remote villages, quiet roads, and scenic landscapes—which are not always served by frequent or extensive public transport systems. That said, Dordogne does offer some public transport choices, particularly for those staying in or traveling between the larger towns.

Buses:

Public buses provide the most common form of transport for getting around the region. Dordogne's bus network is primarily focused on connecting larger towns to nearby villages, but buses are generally infrequent, especially outside of peak tourist season.

• Sarlat, Périgueux, and Bergerac are the main hubs where buses run more frequently, connecting these towns to other places in the region.

• Local buses run between the towns and smaller villages, such as Les Eyzies, Domme, or Rocamadour. However, these services are often limited to specific days or times of the week, so it's important to plan your trip around the schedule.

• Timetables may vary significantly, with fewer buses operating during the winter months or on weekends. Be sure to check schedules in advance, as last-minute changes are common.

Travel Tip: If you plan to rely on buses, keep in mind that the service may not run as frequently as in larger cities. Booking in advance (when possible) or confirming bus times at local tourism offices will ensure a smoother experience.

Taxis & Ride-Hailing:

Taxis are available in the major towns of Dordogne, but they are typically limited in the more rural areas. The availability of taxis can be unpredictable, so it is always best to book in advance if you need a taxi to get around. Ride-hailing apps like Uber are not as prevalent in Dordogne compared to larger cities, so relying on local taxi services is usually your best bet. In smaller villages, you may have to ask around at hotels, restaurants, or local shops to book a taxi.

Travel Tip: If you're not renting a car but need transport to remote villages, you might want to arrange a taxi or private transfer ahead of time, as the bus schedules may not meet your needs.

Trains:

While Dordogne itself does not have a comprehensive train network, the region is well-connected by rail to nearby cities like Bordeaux, Paris, and Limoges. If you're traveling from major cities to Dordogne, taking the train can be an easy and scenic way to arrive.

• The SNCF (French National Railways) offers regular services to and from Bergerac and Périgueux via Bordeaux and other larger cities. From these towns, you can continue your journey by bus or taxi to smaller destinations.

• Bordeaux and Paris are both high-speed train hubs (TGV) with direct access to the Dordogne region. Traveling by train is efficient, especially if you're starting from a major French city. However, once you're in Dordogne, trains don't provide extensive internal connections between the region's smaller towns.

Travel Tip: If you plan to travel by train into Dordogne, consider taking a TGV to Bordeaux or Paris, then switching to local trains or buses for internal travel. Trains can be a great way to start your journey, offering comfort and picturesque views, but for getting around within the region, you'll need to rely on other forms of transport.

Navigating Dordogne without a Car:

While renting a car remains the most convenient way to explore the region, public transport options, though limited, can still get you to key destinations. If you're relying on public transport:

1.   Plan ahead by consulting timetables, especially for bus services.

2.   Consider staying in towns with more frequent connections to surrounding areas, such as Bergerac or Sarlat.

3.   For longer trips to remote villages or rural attractions, you might want to consider private transport options like taxis, bike rentals, or guided tours.

In terms of getting around locally, cycling and walking are excellent alternatives for short distances. Many towns and attractions in Dordogne are close enough for a pleasant walk, and walking through villages like Sarlat-la-Canéda or Domme will allow you to immerse yourself in their charm and history at a leisurely pace.

Conclusion:

Although public transport options in Dordogne may be more limited compared to larger urban areas, there are still plenty of ways to get around. With a bit of planning, you can use buses, taxis, trains, and bikes to explore this picturesque region. However, for the best flexibility and access to all the hidden gems of Dordogne—whether it's ancient castles, lush valleys, or charming villages—a rental car remains your best bet.

Cycling:

Cycling in Dordogne offers a unique and immersive way to experience the region's stunning landscapes, quaint villages, and rolling vineyards. With its serene countryside, quiet backroads, and moderate hills, the Dordogne is ideal for cyclists of all levels, whether you're looking for a leisurely ride or an active adventure.

Cycling Routes and Scenic Views:

One of the most popular routes is the Voie Verte, a dedicated cycling path that stretches from Bergerac to Sarlat, passing through picturesque vineyards, ancient villages, and beautiful farmland. This flat, well-maintained trail offers an easy and scenic ride, ideal for beginners or families looking to enjoy the countryside at a relaxed pace.

For those seeking more of a challenge, Dordogne has a network of hilly backroads that wind through the region's lush forests, riversides, and dramatic limestone cliffs. You'll pass by medieval castles, prehistoric sites, and charming villages that are often only accessible by bike or foot. The Vélo-Route, which connects some of the region's top sights, including Domme, Beynac-et-Cazenac, and La Roque-Gageac, is another wonderful option for those who prefer a more vigorous ride.

Bike Rentals and Facilities:

Local bike rental shops are easily found in towns like Sarlat and Bergerac, where you can choose from a variety of bikes suited to the terrain. Whether you prefer a standard bike for a leisurely ride or an electric bike for tackling those hilly stretches with ease, there's a rental option for everyone. Many rental services also offer guided bike tours, where you'll be led by a local guide who can share the hidden gems of Dordogne and offer insights into the region's history, culture, and natural beauty.

Cycling and Vineyards:

Dordogne's vineyards are a major attraction for visitors, and cycling is one of the best ways to explore them. The routes that run through Bergerac and Monbazillac are particularly popular among cyclists and wine lovers alike. You can stop at local wineries for tastings and tours, discovering some of the region's most celebrated wines, including Bergerac, Monbazillac, and Pecharmant. Cycling from vineyard to vineyard allows you to sample wine in a relaxed, scenic environment, without worrying about driving.

Cycling Tips for Dordogne:

1.   Prepare for Hills: While some paths are flat, Dordogne's rolling hills mean that you'll encounter some climbs along the way. If you're not accustomed to hilly terrain, consider renting an electric bike to make your journey more comfortable.

2.   Stay Hydrated: The region can get hot in the summer, so bring water along, especially on longer rides.

3.   Pack Light: Carry only essentials like sunscreen, snacks, and a map. Many bike rental companies provide secure storage for your belongings if needed.

4.   Respect Local Roads: While cycling, always be cautious on smaller roads, as some can be narrow and winding. Also, be mindful of local traffic, especially around market days and festivals.

5.   Cycle-Friendly Accommodations: Many hotels, guesthouses, and B&Bs in Dordogne are cycle-friendly and offer secure bike storage, laundry services, and helpful local recommendations.

Conclusion:

Cycling through Dordogne offers an exceptional way to connect with the region's natural beauty and heritage. Whether you are gliding past vineyards, exploring medieval towns, or taking in breathtaking views, the freedom and flexibility of cycling make it an unforgettable experience. With plenty of bike rental options and well-marked routes, Dordogne is a cyclist's paradise waiting to be explored.

CHAPTER 4: TOP DESTINATIONS IN DORDOGNE

Medieval Villages

Dordogne is renowned for its medieval villages, each a living testament to the region's rich history, enchanting architecture, and timeless beauty. These villages, often perched on hillsides or nestled along rivers, offer visitors a step back in time, with narrow cobblestone streets, ancient stone houses, and impressive landmarks. Among these, Sarlat-la-Canéda stands out as one of the most captivating and well-preserved medieval towns in France.

Sarlat-la-Canéda: The Jewel of Dordogne

Sarlat-la-Canéda, often simply known as Sarlat, is a place where history, culture, and gastronomy collide in an extraordinary way. The town's well-preserved medieval architecture, including its iconic honey-colored stone buildings, transports you to another era, making it one of the most beautiful towns in France. As one of Dordogne's top destinations, Sarlat offers an authentic experience of rural France that will captivate history lovers, architecture enthusiasts, and travelers seeking a taste of provincial life.

Historical Charm and Architecture

Walking through Sarlat is like stepping into a living museum. The town has maintained its medieval character remarkably well, with a wealth of Renaissance-era buildings, Gothic churches, and medieval mansions lining its winding streets. The most iconic feature is the Place de la Liberté, a central square surrounded by stunning facades that have stood the test of time. Don't miss the Sarlat Cathedral (Saint-Sacerdos Cathedral), a beautiful example of Gothic architecture, with its soaring spires and intricate carvings.

The cobbled streets, lined with quaint shops, cafés, and galleries, add to the charm, making it one of the most picturesque towns in France. Sarlat's commitment to preserving its heritage has earned it a spot as a classified historic town, ensuring that the authenticity and character remain unchanged for generations to come.

Weekly Markets and Gastronomic Delights

Sarlat is especially famous for its weekly market, which takes place on Wednesdays and Saturdays. The market is a true celebration of Dordogne's rich agricultural heritage, offering visitors the chance to sample and purchase the finest local produce, including truffles, foie gras, cheeses, and fresh fruits. The market atmosphere is lively, with vendors proudly displaying their goods and inviting customers to savor the flavors of the region. For food lovers, this is a must-do experience.

In addition to the market, Sarlat is home to a wealth of excellent restaurants, many of which specialize in local cuisine. You can dine on duck confit, truffle-infused dishes, and other regional specialties, all paired with fine local wines. Sarlat also has several bakeries and patisseries where you can indulge in freshly baked canistrelli biscuits or a warm slice of tarte Tatin.

Cultural Events and Festivals

Throughout the year, Sarlat hosts various cultural events and festivals that celebrate the town's history, gastronomy, and heritage. One of the most significant is the Sarlat International Film Festival, which takes place every autumn and attracts filmmakers and cinema enthusiasts from all over the world. The town also hosts medieval fairs, gastronomic festivals, and music events, creating an ongoing vibrant cultural scene.

Exploring the Surroundings

While the town itself is a sight to behold, the surrounding countryside offers its own set of wonders. Just outside of Sarlat, you'll find Château de Beynac, one of the most impressive castles in the Dordogne region, perched high above the Dordogne River. You can also visit the nearby La Roque-Gageac, a stunning village built into the cliffs along the river. From here, take a boat ride along the Dordogne River, which offers spectacular views of the lush landscapes and medieval villages.

For those interested in prehistoric history, the famous Lascaux Caves, with their world-renowned cave paintings, are just a short drive away, making Sarlat an excellent base for exploring the region's rich historical and cultural sites.

Conclusion

Sarlat-la-Canéda is a town that encapsulates the charm and beauty of Dordogne. With its medieval architecture, bustling markets, and exceptional culinary scene, it is a destination that will leave visitors enchanted. Whether you're wandering through its ancient streets, indulging in local delicacies, or enjoying the surrounding natural beauty, Sarlat offers a timeless French experience that should be at the top of any Dordogne itinerary.

Domme: A Bastide Town with Breathtaking Views

Nestled atop a limestone cliff, the charming bastide town of Domme is a true gem of the Dordogne region, offering visitors stunning views of the surrounding countryside and the Dordogne River below. With its medieval origins, cobblestone streets, and historic architecture, Domme is a place where the past and present come together in perfect harmony. Known for its exceptional panoramic views, peaceful atmosphere, and well-preserved heritage, Domme provides a tranquil escape for those looking to experience the quintessential beauty of southwestern France.

A Bastide Town with History and Charm

Founded in 1281 by King Philip III of France, Domme is one of the many bastide towns (fortified medieval towns) that dot the Dordogne region. The town was strategically built on a hill to offer protection against invaders, and it retains much of its original defensive architecture, which adds to its historical allure. As you wander through Domme, the ancient ramparts, gateways, and towers offer glimpses into the town's medieval past.

One of the key features of Domme is its impressive Place de la Halle, a bustling square surrounded by half-timbered houses and arcades. This lively square was once the heart of commerce, and today it remains a charming place to relax and soak in the ambiance of the village. The town's 18th-century church is another must-see landmark, with its classic French architecture and serene atmosphere.

Breathtaking Views of the Dordogne River

One of Domme's most remarkable features is its panoramic views of the Dordogne River and the surrounding landscape. The town's elevated position provides an incredible vantage point, where visitors can take in sweeping views of the river winding through the valley below, the lush greenery of the surrounding forests, and the distant hills of the Perigord Noir. The Promenade des Platanes, a shaded walkway lined with plane trees, offers one of the best spots for taking in these breathtaking vistas. The views are particularly magical at sunrise or sunset, when the changing light casts a soft glow over the river and the village.

Exploring Domme's Secret Underground Cave

While the views from the town's heights are captivating, there's also an intriguing underground element to Domme. Beneath the town lies a series of caves that were once used as storage spaces and even as a refuge during times of conflict. Today, visitors can explore these caves, which include mysterious underground chambers and carved stone passageways that tell a hidden story of the town's past. The caves are open for guided tours, where visitors can learn about Domme's history as a fortified stronghold and discover fascinating secrets about the town's subterranean world.

Cultural Events and Festivals

Like many towns in the Dordogne, Domme is not just about history and scenery—it's also a place where the community comes alive with festivals and events throughout the year. One of the most popular events is La Fête de la Musique, a nationwide celebration of music that takes place every summer. In Domme, local musicians perform in the town square and around the village, filling the streets with music and creating a lively atmosphere.

In addition, Domme hosts various art exhibitions and traditional markets, where visitors can sample local produce and purchase handcrafted goods. The town also celebrates historical reenactments, showcasing the medieval past with costumed actors and dramatic performances.

Outdoor Adventures and Nature

For those who enjoy outdoor activities, Domme's location in the heart of the Dordogne region provides plenty of opportunities to connect with nature. The Dordogne River is ideal for kayaking, canoeing, and boat trips, offering a unique way to explore the valley and admire the surrounding cliffs from the water. Hiking enthusiasts will appreciate the nearby forest trails and walking routes, which wind through the rolling hills and countryside, providing spectacular views at every turn.

Additionally, Domme is part of the Causses du Quercy Regional Natural Park, a vast area of protected natural beauty. The park offers opportunities for birdwatching, wildflower spotting, and exploring diverse ecosystems, from limestone plateaus to lush river valleys.

Conclusion

With its medieval charm, stunning views of the Dordogne River, and rich history, Domme is a destination that combines natural beauty with a fascinating past. Whether you're wandering its cobbled streets, enjoying the panoramic vistas, or discovering the secrets hidden beneath the town, Domme is a place where time slows down, inviting you to relax, explore, and immerse yourself in the serene atmosphere of the Dordogne. This tranquil bastide town is a perfect stop on your journey through the region, offering both beauty and history in equal measure.

La Roque-Gageac: A Picturesque Village Against a Cliff

Nestled at the foot of a towering cliff along the Dordogne River, La Roque-Gageac is one of the most beautiful villages in the region, a living postcard of medieval charm and natural beauty. Its cliffside location provides stunning views of the river below, while the village's traditional stone houses, winding streets, and unique troglodyte dwellings (cave homes) transport visitors to a time long past. As one of the Les Plus Beaux Villages de France (The Most Beautiful Villages of France), La Roque-Gageac is an unmissable stop for travelers seeking both history and scenery in the Dordogne.

A Unique Setting: Carved Into the Cliff

The village's most striking feature is its dramatic location. Perched on the cliffside of a hill, La Roque-Gageac seems to have grown organically out of the rocks, its stone buildings climbing upward along the base of the cliff. Many of the homes and buildings are built into the limestone cliffs themselves, with caves and troglodyte dwellings carved into the rock. These homes, often with stone facades and thatched roofs, give La Roque-Gageac a timeless and fairytale-like atmosphere.

The troglodyte dwellings of La Roque-Gageac were originally carved by local people centuries ago to provide shelter and protection from the elements. These dwellings, some of which are still in use today, showcase the ingenious ways in which the locals adapted to the environment, creating homes that blended seamlessly with the surrounding cliffs. A visit to these caves offers a fascinating glimpse into the region's ancient lifestyle and sustainable living practices.

Exploring the Village Streets

Walking through the narrow, cobbled streets of La Roque-Gageac feels like stepping back in time. The quaint stone houses, some of which date back to the medieval period, line the streets like something from a fairy tale, with their tiled roofs and flower-filled windows. As you explore the village, you'll encounter hidden courtyards, archways, and old stone fountains, each adding to the charm and mystery of this picturesque town.

The heart of La Roque-Gageac is its main street, where you'll find small shops selling local crafts, artisan goods, and fresh produce. The village is home to a handful of restaurants and cafés, where visitors can enjoy regional specialties while soaking in the stunning views of the Dordogne River.

Stunning Views and River Activities

One of the best ways to experience the beauty of La Roque-Gageac is from the river. The Dordogne River flows right past the village, and taking a gabarre boat ride is a great way to admire the village's unique setting against the cliffs. These traditional wooden boats, once used for transporting goods, now offer leisurely rides that provide a different perspective on the village, the surrounding countryside, and the dramatic cliffs.

The river also offers opportunities for other water activities, such as kayaking and canoeing. Paddling along the Dordogne River allows you to take in the scenic beauty of the village and its surroundings from the water, with views of rocky cliffs, lush greenery, and the occasional glimpse of wildlife.

La Roque-Gageac's Historic Treasures

La Roque-Gageac is not only stunning in terms of its setting, but it also boasts several historic landmarks. Among the most notable is the 14th-century Church of Saint-Sauveur, a simple but beautiful Romanesque structure that stands as a testament to the village's deep roots in history. The church's serene atmosphere and quaint charm make it a peaceful stop during a stroll through the village.

Nearby, you can also explore the Fortified House of the Lords of Gageac, a medieval mansion that once served as the residence of the village's noble family. Though it is now a private property, its architectural features and the surrounding village walls offer a glimpse into the region's medieval past.

La Roque-Gageac's Gardens and Walking Trails

Beyond the village itself, La Roque-Gageac is surrounded by natural beauty. The hillside gardens of the village are a perfect spot for relaxation, offering peaceful views over the river and cliffs. A stroll through the Moulin de la Rouzique garden allows visitors to appreciate the diversity of the region's flora while enjoying the peaceful sounds of nature.

For those interested in exploring further, La Roque-Gageac is located within easy reach of several walking trails that wind through the surrounding countryside. Hiking through these trails offers visitors an opportunity to experience the Dordogne's natural beauty up close, from dense woodlands and vineyards to the breathtaking cliffs and riverbanks.

A Rich History and Cultural Significance

La Roque-Gageac's historical significance goes beyond its medieval and prehistoric roots. The village has long been a strategic location due to its protection by the cliffs and its proximity to the river. Throughout the centuries, it has witnessed the ebb and flow of the region's rich cultural and military history.

Today, La Roque-Gageac is a haven for those who wish to escape the hustle and bustle of modern life while soaking in the region's rich heritage. The village is a living museum, where history is tangible, from the troglodyte caves to the medieval architecture that dots the landscape.

Conclusion

With its dramatic cliffside setting, fascinating troglodyte dwellings, and stunning river views, La Roque-Gageac stands as one of the most scenic villages in the Dordogne. This enchanting village offers visitors an opportunity to explore a place where natural beauty and history intertwine, creating a timeless experience. Whether you're wandering through its ancient streets, enjoying a boat ride along the Dordogne River, or simply soaking in the views, La Roque-Gageac promises a journey into the heart of the Dordogne's past and present.

Château de Beynac: A Majestic Fortress Overlooking the Dordogne River

Perched high above the Dordogne River, Château de Beynac stands as one of the most imposing and stunning medieval castles in the region. Its strategic location on a steep limestone cliff offers breathtaking views of the surrounding countryside, making it a must-visit for history enthusiasts and those seeking to experience the grandeur of medieval France.

A History Steeped in Legends

Dating back to the 12th century, Château de Beynac is one of the best-preserved castles in the Dordogne, with a rich history that spans the Hundred Years' War, the French Revolution, and beyond. Originally built by the Beynac family, the castle's rugged exterior tells the story of centuries of conflict, power struggles, and dynastic feuds.

The castle played a pivotal role during the Hundred Years' War as it stood as a fortress defending the region against English invaders. Its commanding position on the river made it a vital stronghold, and its battlements, defensive towers, and moat all attest to its military significance. The castle was strategically located to control the river valley and the lands surrounding it, providing a safe haven for the lords of Beynac and their allies.

As you approach the castle from below, its stone walls, which seem to emerge organically from the cliffside, create a dramatic silhouette against the sky. This imposing architecture has made Château de Beynac a symbol of medieval strength and resilience.

Exploring the Castle's Interior

Walking through the gates of Château de Beynac feels like stepping back in time. Inside, the castle is divided into several levels, each revealing its medieval charm and historical significance. The keep, the oldest part of the castle, rises high above the surrounding land, offering panoramic views of the Dordogne valley and the villages below.

The interior of the castle is a remarkable blend of medieval architectural features and restored rooms. Visitors can explore the grand hall, where battles were planned and important decisions made, and wander through the castle's living quarters, which reveal how the nobility once lived in this stronghold. The kitchen and stables provide further insight into the daily life of the castle's inhabitants, while the chapel adds an element of spiritual significance to the site.

One of the most striking features of Château de Beynac is its defensive architecture. The fortified towers and battlement walkways allow visitors to walk in the footsteps of the soldiers who once defended the castle. The machicolations, the stone overhangs designed to drop stones or boiling oil on enemies, are a testament to the castle's military might.

The Views: A Feast for the Eyes

The views from Château de Beynac are nothing short of spectacular. As you stand atop the ramparts, the Dordogne River winds lazily through the landscape, flanked by dense forests, quaint villages, and rolling hills. The sheer scale of the landscape makes it easy to see why this castle was such an important strategic location. On a clear day, visitors can gaze out across the Dordogne Valley, a patchwork of vineyards, fields, and small stone villages, as well as the iconic Château de Castelnaud on the opposite bank.

The beauty of the surrounding region is enhanced by the dramatic cliffs and riverside scenery, creating a picturesque setting that has attracted artists, photographers, and travelers for generations. Whether you visit in spring, when the countryside is lush and green, or in autumn, when the leaves turn golden and red, the view from the castle remains consistently breathtaking.

The Medieval Dungeon and Towers

One of the more atmospheric parts of the Château de Beynac is the dungeon, located beneath the castle. This dark and mysterious space is where prisoners were once held during the castle's long history. The dungeon adds an element of intrigue and suspense to the castle experience, offering a glimpse into the harsh realities of medieval life. The circular towers that surround the dungeon serve as a reminder of the castle's military function, with their narrow windows designed for defense rather than comfort.

Château de Beynac Today: A Living Legacy

Today, Château de Beynac is not only a historic monument but also a living museum that brings the past to life. The castle is open to the public, offering visitors the opportunity to explore its many rooms and learn about its fascinating history through informative displays, guided tours, and multimedia exhibits. The site regularly hosts historical reenactments and events, allowing visitors to witness the medieval world come to life through costumed actors, demonstrations of medieval crafts, and historical performances.

One of the highlights of a visit to Château de Beynac is the opportunity to experience the castle as part of the larger Dordogne region, with its rich historical tapestry, ancient villages, and natural beauty. The castle itself has been featured in several films, most notably in "The Messenger: The Story of Joan of Arc", bringing its legendary status to an even wider audience.

Conclusion

Château de Beynac is a must-see destination for anyone traveling to the Dordogne region. With its commanding position above the Dordogne River, the castle offers visitors a chance to step back in time and experience the medieval grandeur of this incredible fortress. Whether you're wandering through its stone corridors, gazing at the stunning views, or imagining the battles fought on its ramparts, Château de Beynac provides a window into the history, culture, and beauty of the Dordogne. It is a place where history, landscape, and legend intersect, creating an experience that will leave a lasting impression on all who visit.

Château des Milandes: The Legendary Home of Josephine Baker

Located near the village of Cazeneuve in the Dordogne, the Château des Milandes is not just a beautiful 17th-century château but also the former home of Josephine Baker, one of the most iconic figures of the 20th century. This historic château holds a special place in both French and American history, blending beauty, elegance, and cultural significance into a truly unforgettable experience.

Josephine Baker's Legacy

Josephine Baker, the famous American-born French entertainer and civil rights activist, moved into Château des Milandes in the 1940s. A former ballerina, singer, and dancer, Baker was a celebrated performer in Paris, known for her unique performances that often incorporated themes of freedom, racial equality, and empowerment. In addition to her artistic career, she became a passionate advocate for civil rights and was involved in the French Resistance during World War II.

The château, with its sprawling gardens and majestic surroundings, became her refuge and a place to raise her family. Over the years, she adopted 12 children from different ethnic backgrounds, whom she lovingly referred to as her "Rainbow Tribe." This aspect of her life at Château des Milandes is a central part of the story told at the château today, where visitors can learn about her journey as an artist, activist, and mother.

The Château and Its Gardens

While the historical significance of Château des Milandes is tied to Josephine Baker's life, the château itself is an impressive example of French Renaissance architecture. The building, with its exquisite stonework, towers, and elegant turrets, exudes charm and grandeur. Visitors can explore the interior of the château, which has been carefully restored and furnished with a blend of period furniture and artifacts related to Baker's life and career.

Outside, the gardens of the château are equally as captivating, offering a serene setting with a variety of landscapes, including formal gardens, cypress-lined pathways, and scenic views of the surrounding countryside. The swimming pool and orchard provide a glimpse into the lifestyle that Josephine Baker led during her time at the château. The gardens are also home to a small aviary and a petting zoo, making the château a family-friendly destination.

The château is a place where you can admire the beauty of the French countryside, learn about the life of one of the most important figures in entertainment history, and experience the sense of refuge and legacy that Baker left behind.

Château de Castelnaud: A Fortress with a View and Interactive History

Perched on a cliffside above the Dordogne River, Château de Castelnaud is an extraordinary medieval fortress that offers a glimpse into the past, particularly the medieval warfare that defined the region. The castle is not only an iconic landmark of the Dordogne but also a fascinating interactive museum that brings the history of the Hundred Years' War and medieval combat to life.

A History of War and Rivalry

Built in the 12th century, Château de Castelnaud has witnessed centuries of military conflict and strategic importance. Situated on a rocky outcrop, the castle's position was ideal for defense, controlling both the Dordogne River and the surrounding lands. The château became embroiled in the conflicts of the Hundred Years' War, and its history is closely tied to the rivalry between the French and English forces.

The castle has undergone significant renovations over the years, and it has been preserved as an authentic representation of a medieval fortress, offering a unique opportunity for visitors to understand how these grand castles were designed for defense and warfare. The stronghold is renowned for its battle-ready architecture, including drawbridges, moats, and fortified walls, all of which are integral to the castle's interactive exhibits.

Interactive Museum on Medieval Warfare

What sets Château de Castelnaud apart from other historic sites in the Dordogne is its immersive museum experience. The château houses one of the most extensive collections of medieval weaponry and armour in France, providing a deep dive into the world of siege warfare and medieval combat. Visitors can learn about the mechanics of catapults, crossbows, and longbows, and see full-scale replicas of medieval weapons in action.

In addition to its impressive collection of armor, the castle also features interactive exhibits that allow visitors to engage with medieval battle tactics and defense strategies. For those fascinated by the history of siege warfare, there are demonstrations of catapults and trebuchets, showing how these ancient machines were used to breach castle walls. These exhibits give visitors the chance to step into the shoes of soldiers who once fought for control of such fortresses.

The View from Château de Castelnaud

While the history and museum are compelling, the view from Château de Castelnaud is equally spectacular. Standing at the top of the fortress, you can take in panoramic views of the Dordogne River, the village of Castelnaud-la-Chapelle, and the surrounding wooded hillsides. The scenic vistas offer a chance to understand the strategic importance of the castle's position, as its view commanded all of the surrounding land.

For many, the view of the Château de Beynac on the opposite bank of the river is a highlight, with the two castles once locked in a rivalry during the Hundred Years' War. From the castle's ramparts, you can see the Dordogne Valley stretch out beneath you, a lush landscape dotted with villages, farms, and vineyards.

Visiting Château de Castelnaud

Today, Château de Castelnaud is open to the public year-round, and it remains one of the most visited castles in the Dordogne region. The combination of its historical importance, stunning views, and engaging exhibits makes it an essential stop for anyone interested in medieval history and the culture of the Dordogne.

Visitors can wander through the castle's stone halls, explore its defensive towers, and learn about the events that shaped the region's past. The interactive displays and hands-on experiences make this a family-friendly destination, where even young children can engage with history in a fun and educational way. Whether you're a history buff or simply someone looking to experience the grandeur of a medieval fortress, Château de Castelnaud promises an unforgettable experience.

Prehistoric Sites of Dordogne: A Journey Back in Time

Dordogne is not only renowned for its medieval villages and châteaux, but it also offers a profound connection to the ancient past, showcasing some of the most important prehistoric sites in Europe. With its rich heritage of cave art, archaeological findings, and early human settlements, Dordogne invites visitors to explore the distant worlds of our ancestors. The region is home to some of the most significant prehistoric caves and archaeological sites, including the iconic Lascaux Caves and Les Eyzies-de-Tayac-Sireuil, often considered the world capital of prehistory.

Lascaux Caves: The Birthplace of Prehistoric Art

The Lascaux Caves are undoubtedly one of the most famous prehistoric sites in the world. Located in the Vézère Valley, near the village of Montignac, these caves contain some of the most remarkable and well-preserved examples of prehistoric cave art, dating back over 17,000 years. The caves were discovered in 1940, and since then, they have become a key focal point for both archaeologists and tourists seeking a glimpse into early human life.

The Art of Lascaux

The walls of the Lascaux Caves are adorned with an incredible array of paintings and engravings, depicting animals such as bison, stags, horses, and auroch. These masterpieces are not just stunning works of art but also hold great cultural significance, offering a glimpse into the spiritual and everyday lives of the Paleolithic people who created them. The paintings are done in rich ochre tones, showcasing remarkable skill and understanding of both their surroundings and the animals they depicted.

The Lascaux IV replica cave, located near the original site, offers visitors a chance to experience this extraordinary art without the risk of damaging the fragile original caves. The replica, completed in 2016, is an exact reconstruction of the original cave and provides a state-of-the-art immersive experience. Through cutting-edge technology, visitors can explore the intricate cave art and gain insight into the techniques used by prehistoric artists. Lascaux IV offers a guided tour that provides historical context, helping visitors understand the symbolism and significance of the artwork within its cultural and religious context.

Lascaux: A Symbol of Prehistoric Culture

The Lascaux Caves are more than just paintings—they are a powerful reflection of early human life. The caves are believed to have been used for ritualistic purposes, possibly related to hunting magic or spiritual beliefs. The detail and scale of the paintings suggest that those who created them had an advanced understanding of their environment, showcasing not only the importance of animals in their lives but also a deep connection to the land. Today, the Lascaux caves remain a UNESCO World Heritage site and continue to be one of the most visited and studied prehistoric locations in the world.

Les Eyzies-de-Tayac-Sireuil: The World Capital of Prehistory

Located just a short distance from the Lascaux Caves, Les Eyzies-de-Tayac-Sireuil is often referred to as the world capital of prehistory due to its unparalleled concentration of prehistoric sites and museums. This picturesque village in the Dordogne sits in the heart of the Vézère Valley, a region that boasts a wealth of archaeological discoveries. Les Eyzies has been continuously inhabited for thousands of years, making it a vital link to understanding the early human past.

The Prehistoric Sites of Les Eyzies

Les Eyzies-de-Tayac-Sireuil is home to a number of prehistoric caves, rock shelters, and archaeological digs, which have revealed important artifacts and evidence of early human occupation. The village itself is built against the cliffs of the valley, with some of its houses constructed into the rock faces, resembling troglodyte dwellings. The Vézère Valley is a designated UNESCO World Heritage site, due to its exceptional concentration of Paleolithic sites.

Visitors can explore some of the key prehistoric sites in the area, including the Grotte de Font-de-Gaume, one of the few caves in the region that still contains original paintings. The Grotte de la Micoque is another significant site, where tools dating back to 300,000 years ago were discovered, shedding light on the early Homo sapiens and Neanderthal populations that once inhabited the region.

Museums and Exhibits

For those looking to deepen their understanding of the prehistoric period, Les Eyzies is home to several world-class museums. The Musée National de Préhistoire, located in the heart of the village, is one of the most important archaeological museums in France. The museum features an extensive collection of artifacts—including tools, bones, and carvings—that were discovered in the Vézère Valley. Visitors can view interactive exhibits detailing the prehistoric period, the Paleolithic era, and the development of early human cultures.

One of the museum's most impressive features is its replica of prehistoric cave paintings, which allow visitors to experience the art of our ancient ancestors without the risk of damage to the original sites. The museum also offers educational workshops, giving visitors a hands-on experience of what life may have been like for prehistoric people.

The Experience of Prehistory

For those interested in experiencing prehistory up close, the region offers guided tours that include visits to prehistoric caves, rock shelters, and archaeological digs, where experts share their knowledge of the history and techniques used by our early ancestors. Walking through the valley's stunning landscapes, visitors can imagine what life might have been like for the people who lived here thousands of years ago, hunting and gathering in a world that has long since disappeared.

Conclusion: A Journey to the Dawn of Human History

Dordogne's prehistoric sites are not only some of the most significant in Europe but also offer a window into the earliest forms of human expression and civilization. The region's cave art, archaeological discoveries, and well-preserved prehistoric sites provide a unique opportunity to connect with a past that stretches back millennia. Whether visiting the Lascaux Caves and their magnificent replicas or exploring the rich archaeological landscape of Les Eyzies-de-Tayac-Sireuil, Dordogne offers a fascinating glimpse into the distant past, inviting travelers to step back in time and discover the roots of human culture.

Natural Beauty of Dordogne: Exploring the Dordogne River

Dordogne is a region where the harmony between nature and history creates a breathtaking landscape, and at the heart of this lies the Dordogne River. This winding, tranquil waterway serves as the lifeblood of the region, carving through its valleys, surrounding medieval villages, and lush green hills. The Dordogne River provides the perfect opportunity for those seeking to connect with nature in an authentic way, offering a variety of outdoor activities that allow visitors to experience its serene beauty from a unique perspective.

The Dordogne River: A Lifeline of the Region

The Dordogne River is a major feature of the landscape, stretching across the region, from the Auvergne mountains to the southwest of France. Its meandering waters reflect the soft curves of the land, passing through wooded hills, rugged cliffs, and gentle valleys dotted with ancient villages and châteaux. The river's peaceful flow is contrasted by its historical significance, as it has long been central to the development of the surrounding communities. From prehistoric times to the present day, the river has shaped the area, providing a route for trade, a source of water, and a place for relaxation.

The Dordogne River is particularly famous for its picturesque scenery, and a visit to the region would not be complete without immersing yourself in the beauty of the riverbanks. The landscape here is often described as timeless and idyllic, with the gentle flow of the river juxtaposed against the dramatic cliffs and castles that rise above it. The river is surrounded by an array of floral and fauna, with a combination of dense woodlands, meadows, and vineyards enhancing the natural beauty of the area.

Canoeing and Kayaking: A Peaceful Journey Through Nature

One of the best ways to experience the Dordogne River is by canoeing or kayaking. The river's calm waters make it ideal for these activities, which allow visitors to get close to nature, all while enjoying the stunning views of the surrounding countryside. Paddling along the river's course is an opportunity to disconnect from the world and immerse yourself in the tranquility of the region.

For those new to kayaking or canoeing, there are plenty of guided tours and rentals available at various points along the river. These tours range from easy-going excursions that last just a few hours to more challenging trips that cover several days. Paddling along the river provides an up-close view of the cliffs, medieval villages, and wildlife, such as herons, kingfishers, and even otters, all of which make their home along the riverbanks. The leisurely pace allows for a serene exploration of the Dordogne's unique natural landscape.

For more experienced kayakers or those seeking a more adventurous experience, the river offers stretches of gentle rapids that provide just enough excitement without compromising the peaceful surroundings. Many operators offer self-guided trips, giving visitors the flexibility to explore the river at their own pace, stopping to rest in charming villages or hidden coves along the way.

Boat Tours: Exploring the River with Ease

If you prefer a more relaxed way to take in the stunning views of the Dordogne River, boat tours are an excellent option. These tours offer a leisurely way to appreciate the region's natural beauty and explore parts of the river that are otherwise inaccessible. A variety of boat tours are available, ranging from small electric boats to larger guided cruises, each offering a chance to sit back and enjoy the peaceful atmosphere of the river. These boat rides often take visitors through the heart of the Dordogne Valley, allowing for a panoramic view of the majestic cliffs, woodlands, and villages.

Many boat tours also include stops at key attractions along the river. Visitors may have the opportunity to explore medieval castles, caves, and vineyards nestled along the riverbanks. Boat tours are especially popular for those who want to enjoy the stunning views of places like Château de Beynac, La Roque-Gageac, and Domme from the water. In addition to their historical appeal, these village and château views look particularly enchanting when seen from the water, providing a new perspective on the beauty of Dordogne.

During the warmer months, the boat tours become even more enchanting, with the early morning mist and golden sunlight creating a magical atmosphere as you glide along the river. For those looking for a more romantic experience, some operators offer sunset cruises, where you can enjoy a glass of wine while watching the changing colors of the landscape as the sun dips below the horizon.

Swimming and River Beaches: A Refreshing Experience

For visitors looking for a more active way to enjoy the river, swimming is another popular activity along the Dordogne River. There are several designated beach areas and swimming spots along the river, particularly around Cenac et St. Julien, Sarlat, and Castelnaud-la-Chapelle. These spots offer clear waters for a refreshing dip while providing a picturesque backdrop of the surrounding countryside.

The riverbanks often have shallow areas, ideal for families with children, and the surrounding trees offer natural shade for those looking to relax in the sun. The river's relatively slow flow ensures a safe environment for swimming, and many visitors find the cool waters a perfect way to escape the heat during the warmer months. For a more unique experience, there are also opportunities to swim in the river directly from the back of a boat or at certain river beaches where local swimmers gather to cool off.

Fishing: Enjoying the River's Tranquility

The Dordogne River is a popular spot for fishing, attracting both locals and tourists alike. The river is home to a diverse range of fish species, including trout, pike, and carp, making it a haven for anglers. Fishing enthusiasts can try their luck from the riverbank or rent a boat for a more immersive experience. Whether you are a seasoned angler or simply looking to unwind by the water, fishing in the Dordogne provides a peaceful and rewarding way to spend time in the region's natural surroundings.

Many local fishing guides offer boat trips or fishing excursions, where you can receive expert advice and techniques to make the most of your time on the water. For those traveling with children, family-friendly fishing experiences are available, providing an excellent opportunity to introduce young anglers to the sport.

Conclusion: The Dordogne River—A Gateway to Tranquil Exploration

The Dordogne River offers a range of activities that allow visitors to enjoy the region's natural beauty in a peaceful and immersive way. Whether you are canoeing, boating, swimming, or simply enjoying the scenery from the banks, the river provides an intimate connection to the landscape and a deeper understanding of Dordogne's stunning natural environment. The tranquil flow of the river, combined with the historic villages and castles that line its course, makes the Dordogne River an unforgettable part of any visit to this beautiful French region.

The Vézère Valley: A UNESCO-Listed Treasure of Prehistory and Scenic Walks

The Vézère Valley is one of the most remarkable and significant areas in the Dordogne, known not only for its scenic beauty but also for its prehistoric heritage. This UNESCO World Heritage site is renowned for its caves and rock shelters that house some of the world's most significant prehistoric art, providing an extraordinary glimpse into the lives of our ancient ancestors. The valley, which stretches along the Vézère River, is dotted with prehistoric sites, caves, and archaeological wonders that have made it one of the most important places for understanding human history and evolution.

A Journey Through Prehistory

The Vézère Valley is often referred to as the "Cradle of Prehistory", and for good reason. This region is home to more than 25 prehistoric sites, many of which contain cave paintings, engraved drawings, and ancient artifacts that date back more than 20,000 years. The most famous of these sites is the Lascaux Cave, known for its cave paintings, which depict a rich history of animals and early human life. Though the original cave is no longer open to the public to preserve the artwork, a replica of the Lascaux IV cave can be visited in Montignac, allowing visitors to experience the art and wonder of prehistoric life.

Other important sites in the valley include Les Eyzies-de-Tayac-Sireuil, a small town that is home to the National Prehistory Museum and multiple caves such as La Grotte de Font-de-Gaume and La Grotte de Combarelles, where visitors can see remarkable examples of prehistoric engravings and paintings. Les Eyzies itself is a UNESCO World Heritage town, thanks to its prominence in prehistory and its concentration of archaeological sites.

Beyond the caves, the Vézère Valley is also rich in archaeological digs, where visitors can see the remains of early settlements and ancient tools used by the Neanderthals and early Homo sapiens. The valley is not only an outdoor museum but also a living testament to the endurance of humanity through the ages.

Scenic Walks and Hikes

While the Vézère Valley is a treasure trove for history enthusiasts, it is also a region of stunning natural beauty, with hills, forests, and winding rivers that make it ideal for those looking to explore the outdoors. The valley is crisscrossed with scenic walking trails, many of which pass by ancient caves, riverside meadows, and medieval villages, providing hikers with both natural and historical perspectives of the area. Whether you're walking along the riverbanks, through shaded oak forests, or up hills that offer panoramic views, the Vézère Valley is a perfect place to connect with nature and history in one unforgettable experience.

The GR 36 is one of the most popular long-distance trails in the Vézère Valley, taking hikers on a journey through gorges, woodlands, and historic sites. The trail offers a variety of landscapes, with options suitable for both casual walkers and experienced trekkers. Along the way, hikers are treated to stunning views of the river and the surrounding green hills, as well as the occasional glimpse of prehistoric caves and shelters nestled within the cliffs.

For those who enjoy less strenuous walks, there are many local footpaths around the towns of Les Eyzies and Montignac, where you can take a leisurely stroll through charming villages and explore the surrounding countryside. These trails are great for anyone looking to enjoy the fresh air and beautiful scenery of the valley without a long hike.

Perigord Noir: A Scenic Landscape of Forests, Rivers, and Natural Beauty

The Périgord Noir region is one of the most picturesque and captivating areas of Dordogne, offering a stunning blend of forests, rivers, and charming medieval towns. This region, known for its rugged landscapes and deep forests, is a haven for outdoor enthusiasts, especially those who love hiking, cycling, and immersing themselves in nature. The Périgord Noir is a part of the larger Périgord region, which is famed for its natural beauty, rich cultural heritage, and traditional villages.

A Walker's Paradise

For hikers, Périgord Noir offers some of the most beautiful and diverse trails in Dordogne. The Sarlat area, in particular, serves as a gateway to various nature reserves, and forest walks, where you can explore vast tracts of oak, pine, and chestnut forests that are home to an abundance of wildlife. Trails often lead through river valleys, passing alongside the Dordogne and Vézère Rivers, and meandering through picturesque villages with stone houses, narrow streets, and hidden gardens.

The Causse de Périgord is another natural wonder in this region, offering hiking routes through limestone plateaus and gorges, where you can enjoy sweeping views of the Perigordian countryside. The Causse is famous for its wild landscapes, sparse vegetation, and limestone cliffs, offering a more challenging but equally rewarding experience for avid trekkers.

Rivers, Caves, and Canyons

The Périgord Noir region is also home to a rich array of rivers, caves, and canyons that provide ample opportunities for exploration. The Dordogne River and its tributaries, including the Vézère River, offer ideal settings for canoeing and kayaking, allowing you to enjoy the river's calm flow while surrounded by towering cliffs and green hills.

In addition to the rivers, the region's numerous caves offer hidden gems for those looking for a deeper connection with the natural landscape. Many of these caves are decorated with prehistoric art and offer guided tours that take you on a journey through history. A visit to the Grotte de Font-de-Gaume, for instance, offers a rare glimpse at some of the best-preserved cave paintings in Europe.

For more adventurous souls, the gorges of the Vézère and Célé River offer opportunities for rock climbing and canyoning, making the Périgord Noir a favorite for adrenaline seekers.

Conclusion: A Region for Every Adventurer

Whether you're a history lover eager to explore the prehistoric caves of the Vézère Valley or an outdoor enthusiast ready to immerse yourself in the forests, rivers, and landscapes of Périgord Noir, Dordogne offers a vast range of activities and natural beauty that will captivate and inspire. This area is more than just a destination; it is a place to reconnect with nature, history, and the peaceful pace of life. The Vézère Valley and Périgord Noir are perfect for those seeking a holistic travel experience where prehistory, scenic beauty, and outdoor adventures all come together in one unforgettable journey.

CHAPTER 5: WHAT TO DO IN DORDOGNE

Dordogne is a treasure trove of outdoor adventures, offering a wide array of activities for nature enthusiasts and thrill-seekers alike. Whether you're paddling along meandering rivers, hiking through lush valleys, or discovering prehistoric caves, this region invites you to immerse yourself in the natural beauty and rich history of southwestern France.

Canoeing/Kayaking: Paddle Along the Dordogne and Vézère Rivers

The Dordogne and Vézère Rivers are two of the region's most captivating features, winding their way through dramatic landscapes, deep valleys, and past medieval castles. Canoeing and kayaking are some of the best ways to explore this stunning environment, offering a peaceful yet exhilarating way to experience Dordogne's beauty.

• Dordogne River: Canoeing or kayaking on the Dordogne River offers an incredible opportunity to see the region from a unique perspective. As you paddle downstream, you'll pass by lush greenery, towering limestone cliffs, and some of the region's most iconic châteaux, such as the Château de Beynac and the Château de Castelnaud. The gentle flow of the river makes it suitable for both beginners and experienced paddlers. You can choose from leisurely half-day trips to more adventurous full-day journeys. Along the way, stop to explore caves or dip into the crystal-clear waters for a refreshing swim.

• Vézère River: For those seeking a more tranquil experience, the Vézère River offers calm waters that are perfect for a serene paddle. This river, with its dramatic cliff-side views and ancient landscapes, is also rich in prehistoric significance. As you drift along, you may catch glimpses of ancient rock shelters and caves that were home to prehistoric humans thousands of years ago. You can explore the river's peaceful surroundings and enjoy stunning views of the Vézère Valley, a UNESCO World Heritage Site.

Several local companies offer canoe and kayak rentals, and you can even hire guides for informative trips that explore the prehistory and history of the region. For those who prefer guided tours, it's easy to arrange a day trip that combines paddling with visits to nearby archaeological sites and medieval towns.

Hiking: Trails in the Vézère Valley and Périgord Noir

For those who prefer to keep their feet on the ground, Dordogne offers some of the most scenic hiking trails in France. With its diverse landscapes, from dense forests to rugged hills and river valleys, Dordogne is a paradise for outdoor adventurers looking to hike and explore.

•   Vézère Valley: One of the best places to start your hiking journey is the Vézère Valley, known for its prehistory, natural beauty, and fascinating wildlife. The valley is crisscrossed with trails that vary in difficulty, making it an ideal destination for both casual walkers and experienced trekkers. Many trails follow the Vézère River, offering hikers the chance to explore caves and rock shelters, or take in breathtaking views of medieval villages like Les Eyzies-de-Tayac-Sireuil. The GR6 long-distance trail, which traverses this area, takes you through woodlands and limestone cliffs, with options to branch off and explore hidden caves or archaeological sites.

•   Périgord Noir: Another popular area for hiking is Périgord Noir, home to the beautiful town of Sarlat-la-Canéda and the rolling hills and forests of southwestern Dordogne. Trails in this region offer diverse experiences, ranging from forest walks and river-side strolls to more strenuous hilltop hikes. The Causse de Périgord, a limestone plateau, provides hikers with panoramic views of the Périgord countryside, where the land seems to stretch forever, dotted with medieval towns, ancient villages, and isolated farmhouses. For a more immersive experience, consider hiking through the Black

Perigord's oak forests and along cliffside paths that offer sweeping vistas of the surrounding valleys.

Both the Vézère and Périgord Noir regions offer well-marked trails, but it's always advisable to take a local guide or purchase a detailed trail map, as some of the more remote routes can be difficult to navigate without prior knowledge of the area.

In addition to hiking, trekking enthusiasts can explore more challenging paths that take them into natural reserves and higher altitudes for even more spectacular views. The combination of forests, rivers, and ancient towns makes Dordogne an exceptional destination for anyone seeking an active outdoor getaway with plenty of historical and cultural depth.

Other Outdoor Activities in Dordogne

While canoeing and hiking are among the most popular outdoor activities in Dordogne, there are many more ways to immerse yourself in the region's natural beauty.

• Cycling: Dordogne's quiet country roads and vineyard-lined paths make it an ideal region for cycling. The Loire à Vélo trail passes through parts of Dordogne, but the area also has many local cycling routes that wind through medieval towns and picturesque landscapes. Rent a bike in Sarlat, Bergerac, or Les Eyzies, and cycle your way through charming villages and past centuries-old castles. The Perigord Noir's countryside, with its gentle hills and scenic beauty, is particularly perfect for cycling.

• Hot Air Ballooning: For a truly unique experience, take to the skies in a hot air balloon for a bird's-eye view of Dordogne's stunning landscape. You'll float peacefully over the Dordogne River, drifting past the rolling vineyards, medieval villages, and ancient castles that define this beautiful region. This activity offers a serene and magical way to experience Dordogne, and it's often available during the early morning hours when the light is soft and golden.

• Rock Climbing & Caving: For more adventurous outdoor enthusiasts, Dordogne offers plenty of opportunities for rock climbing and caving. The Vézère Valley has dramatic limestone cliffs that provide ideal climbing conditions, while the caves of Dordogne—such as Grotte de Font-de-Gaume—offer exciting opportunities for exploration. Many of these caves feature prehistoric paintings that date back thousands of years, providing both a challenging and historically enriching experience.

Dordogne is a haven for outdoor adventures, with its rivers, valleys, hills, and prehistoric wonders offering an endless array of ways to explore and experience the beauty of this remarkable region. Whether you're paddling through tranquil waters, hiking rugged trails, or cycling along scenic paths, the opportunities to connect with nature and history are boundless.

Caving & Cave Art: A Journey into Dordogne's Prehistoric Past

Dordogne is not only a paradise for outdoor activities, but it also offers an extraordinary opportunity to step back in time through its hidden caves and prehistoric art. The region is home to some of the most remarkable cave systems in the world, many of which house ancient cave paintings that date back tens of thousands of years. For those seeking an immersive and awe-inspiring adventure, exploring these caves—either through guided tours or spelunking expeditions—provides a deeper connection to Dordogne's ancient past.

Lascaux Caves: The Crown Jewel of Prehistoric Art

No visit to Dordogne would be complete without a trip to the Lascaux Caves, one of the most famous and significant prehistoric sites in the world. Discovered in 1940, the Lascaux cave complex is renowned for its incredible cave paintings, which are believed to be over 17,000 years old. These paintings, created by early humans, depict a variety of animals such as bison, horses, and stags, and are thought to have had symbolic or ritual significance.

Due to preservation concerns, the original Lascaux caves are no longer open to the public, but a meticulously crafted replica called Lascaux IV allows visitors to experience these stunning works of art firsthand. The Lascaux IV center offers an immersive experience with life-sized reproductions of the cave's art, enabling visitors to walk through the cave's labyrinth and marvel at the detailed and vivid images that have survived millennia.

In addition to the Lascaux IV replica, Lascaux II (the first replica created) remains a popular destination for visitors who wish to learn more about the significance of these ancient works. The site is located near the town of Montignac, nestled within the beautiful Vézère Valley, making it easily accessible for those exploring the region.

Les Eyzies-de-Tayac-Sireuil: The Prehistoric Capital

Often referred to as the "capital of prehistory," Les Eyzies-de-Tayac-Sireuil is another essential stop for anyone interested in Dordogne's ancient caves. Situated in the heart of the Vézère Valley, this charming village is surrounded by several prehistoric sites, including caves that house some of the earliest evidence of human life.

Among the notable caves in the region are Grotte de Font-de-Gaume and Grotte des Combarelles. Both of these caves contain impressive collections of prehistoric rock art, with Font-de-Gaume being particularly famous for its polychrome (multi-colored) cave paintings, which depict a wide range of animals such as aurochs, bison, and horses. Grotte des Combarelles, on the other hand, is known for its engraved artwork—a unique and fascinating glimpse into the symbolic expressions of early humans.

Access to both Grotte de Font-de-Gaume and Grotte des Combarelles is strictly controlled, and guided tours are required. Booking in advance is recommended as these tours are often in high demand, especially during peak travel seasons.

Spelunking and Limestone Caves

For those seeking more active exploration, Dordogne offers numerous opportunities for spelunking in its many limestone caves. The region's karst terrain—created over millions of years through the erosion of limestone—has resulted in an extensive network of caves and underground passageways, some of which are open for exploration.

One of the most popular cave systems for spelunking is the Grotte de Rouffignac, a vast underground network of tunnels and chambers that can be explored by electric train. The Grotte de Rouffignac is famous for its prehistoric engravings of animals, including mammoths, horses, and ibex, which were created by early humans more than 13,000 years ago. Visitors can see the cave's stunning artwork while learning about the prehistoric people who lived in the region.

For those who prefer to explore on foot, there are a variety of caves in Perigord Noir and surrounding areas that offer guided tours through twisting tunnels and vast underground chambers. Some caves are entirely natural and have remained virtually unchanged for centuries, while others have been developed for tourist exploration, offering a thrilling way to discover Dordogne's hidden underground world.

Practical Tips for Caving and Cave Art Exploration

• Guided Tours: Exploring Dordogne's caves, especially those with prehistoric art, requires a guided tour. These tours provide valuable insight into the historical and cultural significance of the cave paintings and engravings, as well as the geological features of the caves. Tours can last from one hour to several hours, depending on the cave, so be prepared for varying lengths.

•   Reservations: Due to the popularity of some sites like Lascaux and Font-de-Gaume, it's essential to book your tickets in advance, especially during the summer months. Tour spots can fill up quickly, so early reservations are recommended.

•   Safety: For spelunking, it's important to wear appropriate clothing and footwear (sturdy shoes, long pants). Caves can be slippery, and some are more physically demanding than others. Make sure to follow the guide's instructions and stay within designated areas for your safety.

•   Accessibility: While most caves are accessible to those in good physical condition, some caves, especially those in Perigord Noir and Vézère, may have narrow or steep passages that require agility. Make sure to check accessibility options if you have mobility concerns.

•   Respect the Sites: Remember that the caves in Dordogne are protected and have cultural and historical significance. Do not touch the paintings or engravings, and be mindful of your noise levels and actions to help preserve these fragile environments for future generations.

Caving and exploring cave art in Dordogne is a unique journey into the depths of human history. Whether you're marveling at the Lascaux masterpieces or spelunking through the underground passages of the Perigord Noir, the experience offers a connection to a world that is thousands of years old. For any traveler with an interest in prehistoric art, history, or adventure, Dordogne's caves are an essential part of the experience, offering an unforgettable glimpse into the past.

Cultural and Historical Experiences in Dordogne: A Journey Through Time

Dordogne is a region where history and culture intertwine, offering travelers a deep dive into its rich heritage. From its medieval castles and prehistoric caves to its vibrant local markets and cultural events, the Dordogne provides a variety of experiences that allow you to truly understand the soul of this captivating region. Whether you're a history enthusiast, a food lover, or someone seeking to immerse themselves in the region's medieval charm, Dordogne's cultural and historical offerings will surely captivate your senses.

Visit Sarlat's Weekly Market: A Culinary Paradise

One of the most iconic experiences in Dordogne is a visit to Sarlat-la-Canéda's weekly market, a must-see for food lovers and cultural explorers alike. Held every Wednesday and Saturday morning, this bustling market in the heart of Sarlat's medieval town center is a sensory feast. The cobbled streets and ancient stone buildings serve as the perfect backdrop for an array of local produce and handcrafted goods, making it a vibrant and authentic way to experience the flavors of Dordogne.

The market is particularly famous for its fresh, high-quality truffles, which are a local specialty. You'll find vendors selling truffle oils, truffle-infused products, and of course, the prized fresh truffles themselves. Alongside truffles, the market showcases other Dordogne culinary gems, including foie gras, duck confit, and an assortment of local cheeses like Crottin de Chavignol and Ossau-Iraty. The atmosphere is lively, with local producers eager to share their passion for Dordogne's gastronomic heritage. It's the perfect place to sample the region's finest products and perhaps even take home a few souvenirs to recreate the flavors of Dordogne long after your visit.

Aside from food, the market is also a great spot to pick up handmade crafts, including pottery, woven goods, and local artwork, which offer a glimpse into the artistic traditions of the region.

Medieval Fairs: Step Back in Time

For those interested in Dordogne's medieval history, the region offers several opportunities to immerse yourself in its vibrant past through medieval fairs and reenactments. One of the most popular events is the Fête Médiévale in Sarlat, a colorful celebration of the region's medieval heritage. Held every summer, this festival transforms Sarlat into a medieval wonderland, with townspeople donning period costumes and engaging in historical reenactments. Expect to see knights jousting, archers demonstrating their skills, and minstrels playing medieval tunes. The streets come alive with street performers, medieval market stalls, and live demonstrations, offering visitors a fascinating glimpse into daily life during the Middle Ages.

The festival is not only a chance to experience medieval combat and performances but also an opportunity to see medieval crafts being made, from blacksmithing to weaving. The festive atmosphere is infectious, with food stalls offering traditional dishes, including roast meats, stews, and medieval-inspired pastries.

Additionally, many of Dordogne's castles and fortresses host medieval-themed events, such as château tours with historical reenactments or special exhibitions about the region's medieval military history. These experiences add a layer of authenticity to your exploration of Dordogne's historical legacy.

Dordogne's Historical Museums: A Deeper Dive into the Past

Dordogne is a treasure trove of historical sites and museums, where you can gain a deeper understanding of its diverse heritage. Two of the region's most notable museums are dedicated to prehistory and medieval history, offering a comprehensive look at the ancient and medieval eras.

•   The Prehistory Museum in Les Eyzies-de-Tayac-Sireuil: Situated in the Vézère Valley, known as the "capital of prehistory," this museum is a must-visit for anyone interested in the prehistoric past. The museum showcases a vast collection of artifacts, including tools, weapons, and prehistoric art discovered in the local caves. It also provides a fascinating look at the lives of the early humans who inhabited this region more than 40,000 years ago. Visitors can view detailed exhibits about the Neanderthals and Cro-Magnon people, as well as learn about the significance of Dordogne's cave art. The museum's educational displays are complemented by nearby prehistoric sites and cave paintings, allowing visitors to truly connect with the region's ancient past.

•	The Medieval Weapons Museum at Château de Castelnaud: For those fascinated by the medieval era, the Château de Castelnaud offers an exceptional museum experience. Located within the imposing walls of the castle itself, the Medieval Weapons Museum displays a stunning collection of medieval weaponry, including swords, crossbows, armor, and siege equipment. The museum not only focuses on the tools of medieval combat but also delves into the strategies and military history of the period. The castle's viewpoint offers breathtaking views of the surrounding valley, enhancing your historical journey as you learn about the region's role in the Hundred Years' War and other pivotal conflicts of the medieval period.

•	Château de Beynac and Château des Milandes also host historical exhibitions related to their respective histories, offering a deeper understanding of medieval nobility and the French Renaissance.

Cultural Traditions and Local Experiences

Beyond the formal events and museums, Dordogne offers a wealth of other cultural experiences that reflect the region's local traditions and lifestyles. Visitors can explore artisan workshops, where skilled craftsmen create everything from wooden furniture to pottery, preserving centuries-old techniques. In some villages, you may even find local farmers' markets where you can interact with producers of regional specialties, from freshly made goat cheeses to homemade jams and breads.

For a deeper cultural connection, consider visiting a local vineyard to learn about Dordogne's wine-making traditions and perhaps even take part in a wine tasting. The region is known for its red wines, particularly from the Bergerac and Monbazillac areas, and a wine tour is an excellent way to appreciate the flavors and history of the land.

Dordogne's cultural festivals are also a great way to engage with the region's vibrant arts scene, whether it's classical music performances, art exhibitions, or traditional dances. No matter where you are in the region, there's always something cultural to discover.

Dordogne's cultural and historical experiences are a true reflection of the region's rich past and vibrant present. Whether you're indulging in its culinary delights at Sarlat's market, stepping back in time at a medieval fair, or exploring its prehistoric caves and medieval castles, the region offers a journey that appeals to the curious traveler. These experiences will not only immerse you in Dordogne's history and traditions but will also leave you with lasting memories of this timeless and captivating part of France.

Wine & Gastronomy: A Feast for the Senses in Dordogne

Dordogne is a region where food and wine are not just part of the experience; they are central to the very essence of life here. The gastronomy of Dordogne is rich in flavors, rooted in its natural bounty, and shaped by centuries of tradition. From its world-renowned wines to its distinctive regional dishes, the culinary scene in Dordogne offers a true reflection of its rich heritage and vibrant local culture. Whether you are a food lover, a wine enthusiast, or someone looking to engage with the local culinary traditions, Dordogne promises a journey that will tantalize your taste buds.

Wine Tastings: A Journey Through Vineyards

Dordogne is nestled between some of France's most celebrated wine regions, making it a prime destination for wine lovers. The Bergerac and Monbazillac vineyards, located within the region, produce some of the finest wines in France, known for their distinctive flavors and long-standing traditions. Whether you're a connoisseur or a casual wine drinker, a wine-tasting tour in Dordogne is an experience that should not be missed.

• Bergerac is one of the most prominent wine-producing regions in Dordogne, renowned for its red wines made from Merlot, Cabernet Sauvignon, and Cabernet Franc grapes. The region also produces elegant white wines, such as Sémillon and Sauvignon Blanc, that pair perfectly with Dordogne's renowned dishes. The village of Bergerac itself is home to many family-run wineries that offer intimate tours, where you can explore the vineyards, learn about the winemaking process, and, of course, sample the exceptional wines.

•   Monbazillac, famous for its sweet white wines, is another must-visit destination. The Monbazillac AOC (Appellation d'Origine Contrôlée) wine is a late-harvest dessert wine, made primarily from Sémillon, Sauvignon Blanc, and Muscadelle grapes. The region's historic châteaux, such as Château de Monbazillac, offer stunning views of the vineyards and provide guided tours that delve into the history of the wine estate and its winemaking techniques. These tours often end with a tasting of their wines, including the signature Monbazillac wine, which has a rich, honeyed sweetness perfect for pairing with foie gras or a slice of tarte aux noix (walnut tart).

For the ultimate wine experience, consider joining a vineyard tour that will take you through the picturesque landscapes of Dordogne. These tours often include visits to multiple wineries, where you can sample a range of local wines, enjoy breathtaking vineyard views, and learn from passionate winemakers about the unique terroir of the region.

Regional Dishes: Savoring the Flavors of Dordogne

No visit to Dordogne is complete without indulging in its traditional cuisine, which is deeply rooted in the region's agricultural heritage. The flavors of the land are reflected in every dish, using fresh, local ingredients that have been perfected over generations. Here are some of the must-try regional dishes:

•   Foie Gras: Perhaps the most iconic dish of Dordogne, foie gras is made from the liver of a duck or goose and is considered a delicacy in French cuisine. In Dordogne, the dish is served in various forms, including foie gras pâté, pan-fried foie gras, and foie gras terrine. Pair it with a glass of Monbazillac wine for a classic Dordogne experience.

•   Confit de Canard: This slow-cooked duck dish is a staple of the Dordogne region. The duck is preserved in its own fat, resulting in tender, flavorful meat that is crispy on the outside and melt-in-your-mouth delicious. It is often served with potatoes, salads, or vegetables.

•   Truffles: Dordogne is famous for its black truffles, often called the "black diamond" of French cuisine. These rare fungi are harvested during the winter months and are used to flavor a variety of dishes, from omelettes and pastas to foie gras and meats. A visit to Dordogne during truffle season (from November to March) offers the chance to experience this prized ingredient in its freshest form, often accompanied by a guided truffle hunt led by trained truffle dogs.

•   Walnut-based Desserts: The region is known for its walnuts, which are incorporated into numerous sweet treats, including the rich and nutty tarte aux noix (walnut tart). This dessert is a perfect blend of sweet, earthy, and buttery flavors and is often served with a dollop of crème fraîche or a scoop of vanilla ice cream.

•   Pruneaux d'Agen: Dordogne is also famous for its prunes—dried plums from the region of Agen. These prunes are often used in desserts and sauces but are also enjoyed on their own as a sweet snack.

Cooking Classes: Master the Art of French Cooking

For those who wish to immerse themselves even further in Dordogne's culinary world, taking part in a cooking class is the perfect way to learn how to create traditional French dishes from scratch. Local chefs and culinary schools in Dordogne offer hands-on cooking workshops where you can learn to prepare a variety of dishes, from foie gras to classic French sauces and desserts.

These classes typically begin with a visit to a local market, where you'll shop for fresh, seasonal ingredients, before heading to the kitchen to prepare a full meal under the guidance of an experienced chef. Not only will you learn essential cooking techniques, but you'll also gain a deeper understanding of the region's culinary traditions. At the end of the class, you'll sit down to enjoy the dishes you've prepared, paired with locally sourced wines.

Some cooking schools even offer themed workshops, such as truffle cooking or wine pairing, providing an opportunity to delve deeper into specific aspects of Dordogne's rich gastronomic heritage.

Dordogne's wine and gastronomy is a celebration of flavor, tradition, and local produce. From the world-class wines of Bergerac and Monbazillac to the unforgettable regional dishes that showcase the area's rich culinary heritage, Dordogne offers a gastronomic adventure that will delight all the senses. Whether you're tasting wine at a vineyard, savoring the richness of foie gras, or learning the art of

French cooking, Dordogne invites you to indulge in a culinary experience that is as unforgettable as the region itself.

Shopping in Dordogne: A Treasure Trove of Regional Delights

Shopping in Dordogne is an experience that invites you to slow down and immerse yourself in the local culture, where the products on offer are often made with time-honored methods, passion, and a deep connection to the land. Whether you're hunting for regional delicacies, artisan goods, or vintage treasures, Dordogne's markets, shops, and galleries provide ample opportunities to bring home a piece of this enchanting region.

Local Markets: The Heartbeat of Dordogne

The region's markets are an essential part of its culture and offer a vivid glimpse into the day-to-day life of Dordogne's residents. These lively, open-air markets are the perfect place to discover the freshest local produce, regional specialties, and unique handmade crafts. Visiting one of these markets is not just about shopping—it's about experiencing the spirit of Dordogne.

•   Sarlat Market: Held on Wednesdays and Saturdays, the Sarlat market is one of the most renowned in the region. Set in the heart of the stunning medieval town, this market is an absolute must-visit for any shopper. Stalls overflow with local produce, such as cheeses, truffles, foie gras, cured meats, and freshly baked bread. You'll also find fresh fruit and vegetables from local farms, perfect for preparing a picnic to enjoy along the Dordogne River. For those with a sweet tooth, be sure to try the walnut-based sweets, a regional specialty.

In addition to food, the Sarlat market is a great place to pick up artisanal goods, including pottery, textiles, and handcrafted wooden items, reflecting the skilled craftsmanship of local artisans. The market's location in the medieval center adds an extra layer of charm, as you wander through narrow cobblestone streets while browsing stalls full of vibrant, colorful goods.

• Bergerac Market: Located in the heart of Bergerac, another stunning medieval town, the Bergerac market is equally lively, though it tends to be less crowded than the one in Sarlat, offering a more laid-back shopping experience. Held on Tuesdays and Saturdays, the market features a wonderful selection of gourmet items, from truffle oils and local wines to cured meats and cheeses. Don't miss the opportunity to pick up a bottle of Bergerac wine or the sweet, rich Monbazillac wine, which the region is known for.

• Local Villages: Many smaller towns and villages throughout Dordogne host their own weekly markets, where you can discover more specialized goods. Markets in Domme, La Roque-Gageac, and Les Eyzies feature a selection of artisan breads, homemade jams, and handcrafted wooden toys, as well as more seasonal produce like mushrooms in the autumn and chestnuts in winter.

Artisan Goods and Unique Souvenirs

In addition to the vibrant food markets, Dordogne is home to a wealth of artisanal goods created by skilled local craftspeople. You can find everything from traditional pottery and jewelry to woodwork and hand-woven textiles, often made using techniques passed down through generations.

• Sarlat Art Galleries & Workshops: Sarlat is known for its strong artistic community, and you'll find numerous art galleries and workshops showcasing the work of local artisans. The town's galleries feature works from painters, sculptors, and photographers, often focusing on themes that reflect the beauty and history of Dordogne. Local pottery and ceramics are especially popular, with many shops offering beautifully crafted pieces ranging from rustic bowls and vases to elegant serving dishes. Jewelry crafted from local stones, silver, and wood also makes for a perfect souvenir, often reflecting the natural beauty of the region.

• Crafts in Domme and La Roque-Gageac: Both Domme and La Roque-Gageac are home to talented artisans who work with local materials like wood, stone, and clay. You'll find wooden furniture, carved figurines, and other handcrafted treasures in small workshops scattered throughout these picturesque towns. Keep an eye out for baskets woven from local reeds or leather goods crafted by local artisans.

• Vintage and Antiques: For collectors and lovers of antiques, Dordogne offers a range of antique shops where you can find items that capture the essence of the region's rich history. In towns like Bergerac and Sarlat, you can browse through antique furniture, paintings, jewelry, and silverware. The Antique Quarter in Bergerac is particularly known for its selection of vintage furniture, rustic farm tools, and relics that offer a glimpse into Dordogne's past.

Specialty Stores: Souvenirs with a Local Twist

•   Truffles & Walnut Products: No visit to Dordogne would be complete without a taste of its world-famous truffles. You'll find a number of specialty shops in Sarlat, Bergerac, and Les Eyzies where you can purchase fresh truffles during the season or truffle-infused products, such as truffle oils, truffle salts, and truffle-based sauces. The region is also known for its walnuts, so don't forget to take home a bottle of walnut oil or a pack of walnut sweets.

•   French Wines & Local Spirits: Dordogne is surrounded by some of the best wine-producing regions in France, so it's the perfect place to purchase a bottle (or two) of local wine. Many wineries offer wine-tasting experiences and will have bottles available for sale. If you're in Bergerac or Monbazillac, be sure to pick up a bottle of the region's famous Monbazillac wine. Additionally, you can find specialty liquors, such as Pineau des Charentes, a sweet fortified wine, in local liquor shops.

•   Textiles & Local Crafts: The region is also known for its high-quality textiles, such as handwoven linen and embroidered fabrics. You can find beautiful tablecloths, napkins, towels, and other linens made in traditional designs. Look for vintage fabrics and patchwork quilts in many of the antique and craft stores dotted around the region.

Shopping in Dordogne is far more than just acquiring goods—it's an opportunity to connect with the region's artisans, its traditions, and its history. From exploring the bustling markets of Sarlat and Bergerac to discovering the local art galleries and workshops, shopping here allows you to bring home a piece of Dordogne's soul. Whether you're taking home local delicacies, a piece of handcrafted pottery, or an antique treasure, your purchases will serve as a lasting reminder of this timeless and enchanting region.

CHAPTER 6: ACCOMMODATION OPTIONS IN DORDOGNE

Dordogne is a region that knows how to cater to every traveler's needs, offering a variety of accommodation options that allow you to experience its stunning landscapes, medieval charm, and rich history in the way that suits you best. Whether you're seeking the luxury of a château hotel, the coziness of a boutique hotel nestled in a village, or the intimacy of a gîte or vacation rental, Dordogne has something for everyone. Here's a look at the different types of accommodation you can choose from when exploring this enchanting region.

Luxury Stays: Indulge in the Majesty of Dordogne

For those looking to experience the grandeur of Dordogne's medieval heritage, there is no better way than staying in one of the region's château hotels. These grand castles have been converted into luxurious hotels, offering the ultimate indulgence in history, style, and comfort. Imagine waking up in a bed where royalty once slept, enjoying breakfast in a castle dining room, or sipping wine in the opulent surroundings of a centuries-old estate.

• Château de Montfort: Situated in the picturesque town of La Roque-Gageac, Château de Montfort is a 16th-century château turned luxurious hotel with breathtaking views over the Dordogne River. This château features elegantly decorated rooms, a beautiful garden, and a serene pool overlooking the river. It's the perfect place for anyone wanting to experience the elegance of a bygone era while enjoying modern amenities, including a spa, wine cellar, and fine dining. Staying here makes you feel like part of history itself, with the scenic landscapes of the region adding to the experience.

• Château des Vigiers: Located near Bergerac, Château des Vigiers combines the beauty of the Dordogne countryside with the opulence of a golf resort and spa. This 16th-century château offers stylish rooms and suites, a luxurious spa, and fine dining. Guests can enjoy wine tastings from the vineyard that surrounds the estate, as well as indulge in a round of golf or relax in the tranquil atmosphere. It's a perfect retreat for those seeking peace, relaxation, and a touch of grandeur.

•	Château de Salette: Another gem in the Dordogne is Château de Salette, located near the town of Bergerac. With a history dating back to the 18th century, this château hotel offers guests the chance to experience the elegance of French aristocracy. The property is surrounded by lush gardens and vineyards, and the luxurious rooms provide sweeping views of the Dordogne landscape. The on-site restaurant serves exquisite regional cuisine, and wine enthusiasts will enjoy the chance to sample local wines produced on the estate.

Boutique Hotels: Charming Escapes in Medieval Villages

For those who prefer a more intimate and personalized experience, Dordogne offers a range of charming boutique hotels set in its medieval villages. These smaller, independent hotels often feature unique, stylish decor and exceptional service, giving guests a feel for the region's character and local culture.

•	La Maison de la Comtesse: Located in the heart of Sarlat-la-Canéda, one of the most beautiful medieval towns in the region, La Maison de la Comtesse is an intimate, boutique hotel set within a historic building. The hotel combines modern amenities with the charm of centuries-old architecture, offering rooms that are both comfortable and beautifully appointed. Staying here puts you right at the center of Sarlat's charming streets, making it easy to explore the town's market, restaurants, and medieval landmarks.

• Le Relais de la Malmaison: For a stylish yet cozy stay, Le Relais de la Malmaison in the town of Domme is an excellent choice. This boutique hotel offers a mix of classic elegance and modern touches, with rooms that feature rustic wooden beams and views of the surrounding countryside. The hotel also boasts an outdoor pool, perfect for unwinding after a day of sightseeing. The proximity to Domme's medieval charm and the Dordogne River makes it an ideal place to relax while taking in the region's beauty.

• Les Terrasses de Dordogne: Located in the quaint town of Vitrac, Les Terrasses de Dordogne offers a boutique experience with a peaceful, countryside setting. The hotel is a converted 18th-century house, blending rustic charm with modern comfort. Guests can enjoy panoramic views of the Dordogne Valley from their rooms, and the nearby village is perfect for exploring local cafes, restaurants, and shops.

Gîtes & Vacation Rentals: A Home Away from Home

For a more local and intimate experience, consider renting a gîte (self-catering cottage) or a vacation rental. These accommodations allow you to live like a local and enjoy the region at your own pace, with the flexibility to cook your own meals and explore the countryside at leisure. Many gîtes are located in charming villages or tucked away in the rolling hills of the Périgord Noir region, giving you a tranquil escape from the hustle and bustle.

• Les Gîtes de Saint-Amand: Set in a peaceful rural area near the town of Rocamadour, Les Gîtes de Saint-Amand offers cozy, stone-built cottages that combine traditional charm with modern conveniences. These gîtes are surrounded by stunning nature, making them ideal for hiking, cycling, and outdoor activities. With fully equipped kitchens, private gardens, and comfortable living spaces, these gîtes are perfect for families, couples, or groups of friends looking for a more independent experience.

• La Ferme de Mazières: Located near the village of Vézac, La Ferme de Mazières offers charming holiday rentals on a traditional farm. The stone cottages are nestled in the heart of the Dordogne countryside, offering peace, privacy, and stunning views of the surrounding hills and valleys. Guests can enjoy fresh, local produce and experience life on a working farm, where seasonal vegetables, fruit, and even truffles are grown.

• Dordogne Luxury Villas: For those seeking a higher-end vacation rental, Dordogne offers an array of luxury villas and manor houses that provide top-tier comfort and breathtaking views of the region's landscapes. Many of these properties feature expansive gardens, private pools, and outdoor dining areas, making them ideal for those looking to host a special celebration or family gathering in the heart of the French countryside.

Choosing the Right Accommodation in Dordogne

Dordogne's wide array of accommodation options ensures that every type of traveler will find something that suits their tastes and needs. Whether you're indulging in the grandeur of a château hotel, experiencing the charm of a boutique hotel in a medieval village, or seeking a more intimate and personal stay in a gîte or vacation rental, you'll find that Dordogne offers the perfect base from which to explore its rich history, scenic beauty, and culinary delights. The region's accommodations are not just places to stay—they are integral to your experience of this timeless and captivating part of France.

Camping & Glamping: Embrace Nature in Dordogne

For those seeking a more immersive outdoor experience, camping and glamping in Dordogne offer a unique way to connect with the region's stunning natural beauty. Whether you're pitching a tent by the peaceful Dordogne River or enjoying the luxury of glamping in the heart of Périgord Noir, these options provide the perfect balance of comfort and adventure.

Camping: Embrace the Outdoors

Camping in Dordogne allows you to wake up to the sounds of nature, breathe in the fresh air, and enjoy the simplicity of outdoor life. There are many campsites scattered throughout the region, ranging from basic sites to more luxurious setups, often located near rivers, forests, or scenic villages.

• Camping Le Moulin de David: Located near the town of Sarlat, Le Moulin de David offers a peaceful riverside campsite. Surrounded by lush greenery, this family-friendly site features well-maintained facilities, including heated pools, a playground, and a small café. It's the perfect spot for those who enjoy outdoor activities like canoeing or hiking, with easy access to the Dordogne River and nearby trails.

• **Camping La Plage:** Situated in Vitrac, this campsite lies right on the banks of the Dordogne River, making it ideal for water activities such as swimming, kayaking, and fishing. Guests can camp in spacious, shaded areas or opt for mobile homes with full amenities. The site also offers plenty of opportunities to explore nearby attractions like Castelnaud and Beynac, or enjoy a leisurely day in the region's scenic nature.

• **Camping Les Cigales:** Located in Saint-Cyprien, Les Cigales is a tranquil campsite set amidst the stunning landscape of the Périgord Noir. It's a great base for outdoor lovers, offering direct access to the surrounding nature, hiking trails, and river activities. The site features comfortable pitches for tents, caravans, and motorhomes, as well as a range of amenities, including a swimming pool and restaurant serving local dishes.

Camping in Dordogne gives you the opportunity to stay close to nature while having all the basic comforts you need for a memorable trip. Many campsites also offer eco-friendly options, allowing you to enjoy the landscape while respecting the environment.

Glamping: Luxury Meets Nature

For those who want to experience the great outdoors without sacrificing comfort, glamping (glamorous camping) provides the ideal solution. Glamping sites in Dordogne offer unique, luxurious accommodations that allow you to immerse yourself in nature while enjoying the comforts of home. From safari tents to luxury yurts, glamping in Dordogne combines the charm of camping with the convenience of upscale amenities.

• Domaine des Ormes: Located in Saint-Martin-de-Ribérac, Domaine des Ormes offers a luxurious glamping experience in the heart of the Périgord Vert. Guests can stay in beautifully furnished safari tents or eco-lodges, complete with private bathrooms, comfortable beds, and outdoor terraces. The site also offers a range of activities, from canoeing on the Dronne River to hiking and cycling through the surrounding forest. It's perfect for nature lovers who want to enjoy the region's beauty with a touch of luxury.

• La Maison de la Riviere: Situated along the Vézère River, La Maison de la Riviere offers a glamping experience that combines luxury and tranquility. Guests can stay in beautifully decorated bell tents with comfortable beds, cozy seating areas, and private decks overlooking the river. The site's serene setting is ideal for those looking to disconnect, while still enjoying access to modern amenities, including a hot tub, yoga sessions, and delicious locally sourced meals.

• Les Gîtes de Sarlat - Glamping: If you want to combine the comforts of a traditional glamping site with the opportunity to explore the beautiful town of Sarlat-la-Canéda, consider staying at Les Gîtes de Sarlat. This glamping site offers spacious, furnished tents set in a private garden, where you can unwind after a day of sightseeing. Located just outside the medieval town, it provides the perfect balance of nature and culture, with easy access to local markets, shops, and restaurants.

The Benefits of Camping & Glamping in Dordogne

Camping and glamping in Dordogne offer several advantages:

• Proximity to Nature: Both options allow you to stay close to the region's natural beauty, with many campsites and glamping sites located near rivers, forests, and scenic viewpoints. It's a great way to experience the stunning landscapes of Dordogne, from the winding Dordogne River to the lush hills of the Périgord Noir.

• Affordable Accommodation: Camping is one of the most budget-friendly ways to experience Dordogne. It allows travelers to enjoy the region's beauty without the high cost of hotels. Glamping, while slightly more expensive, provides an affordable yet luxurious alternative to traditional hotels or château stays.

• Outdoor Activities: Many campsites and glamping sites are situated in areas with abundant opportunities for outdoor adventures. Whether you enjoy canoeing, hiking, or cycling, you'll have easy access to activities that allow you to explore Dordogne's natural beauty at your own pace.

• Eco-Friendly Experience: For environmentally conscious travelers, camping and glamping are great ways to reduce your carbon footprint while still enjoying the beauty of the region. Many glamping sites are built with sustainable practices in mind, and campsites are often located in areas that promote eco-tourism.

Conclusion: A Unique Way to Experience Dordogne

Whether you're seeking a back-to-basics camping experience or the comfort and luxury of glamping, Dordogne offers the perfect opportunity to immerse yourself in the region's natural beauty. Camping and glamping give you a unique chance to connect with nature, explore the stunning landscapes, and experience Dordogne in a more authentic and intimate way.

CHAPTER 7: SEASONAL EVENTS & FESTIVALS IN DORDOGNE

Dordogne's vibrant cultural calendar is filled with festivals and events that celebrate the region's rich history, food, music, and traditions. Whether you visit in spring, summer, or winter, there's always something special happening, offering a chance to experience the heart of this captivating region.

Spring and Summer: A Time for Music, History, and Culinary Delights

As the region comes alive with blooming flowers and warm weather, Dordogne hosts a variety of festivals that showcase its diverse cultural heritage. From world-class music performances to lively medieval celebrations, spring and summer are the perfect time to visit if you want to experience the region's festive spirit.

• Sarlat Music Festival (Festival de Musique de Sarlat)

Held annually in Sarlat-la-Canéda, the Sarlat Music Festival is a must-attend for classical music lovers. Typically taking place in June, this festival transforms the medieval town into a grand stage for some of the finest musical performances in the region. Set against the backdrop of Sarlat's historic squares, churches, and courtyards, concerts feature talented musicians from around the world, performing everything from orchestral works to intimate chamber music. The festival's mix of classical and contemporary performances makes it a unique way to immerse yourself in both the culture and the beauty of Dordogne.

• Medieval Festivals: Jousting, Reenactments, and Historical Revelry

Dordogne's medieval past comes to life in a variety of festivals throughout the spring and summer. One of the most notable is the Fête Médiévale in Sarlat, where the town's cobblestone streets are transformed into a medieval village. The festival includes exciting jousting tournaments, traditional music, dancing, and theatrical reenactments of historical battles and feasts. Visitors can watch knights in shining armor compete for glory, stroll through artisan markets offering medieval crafts, and experience what life was like in the Middle Ages. Other towns like Domme and

Beynac-et-Cazenac also host their own medieval festivals, featuring similar festivities that celebrate the region's history and heritage.

• Truffle Festival (January)

Though it takes place in the colder month of January, the Truffle Festival in Sarlat is a key event for food enthusiasts. This annual celebration highlights one of Dordogne's most prized culinary treasures – the Périgord truffle. Visitors can learn about the art of truffle hunting, sample various truffle-based dishes, and purchase fresh truffles from local producers. The festival also features workshops, cooking demonstrations, and tastings, allowing you to deepen your appreciation for this aromatic, highly sought-after ingredient. If you're in Dordogne in winter, this festival is a perfect introduction to the region's rich food culture.

• Fête de la Musique (June 21st)

Part of a nationwide celebration, Fête de la Musique is held every year on June 21st in towns and villages across France, including Dordogne. Local musicians take to the streets, squares, and parks to perform free concerts, making this a fun and lively event for visitors of all ages. Whether you enjoy jazz, rock, classical, or folk music, the Fête de la Musique brings together a wide array of musical styles, creating a festive atmosphere in towns like Sarlat, Bergerac, and Perigueux.

Autumn and Winter Festivals in Dordogne

As the leaves turn golden and the air grows crisp, Dordogne's autumn and winter festivals bring a warm, festive spirit to the region. These seasons in Dordogne are a celebration of harvests, traditions, and the cozy charm of village life. Whether you're savoring the last days of autumn or immersing yourself in the winter holiday spirit, these seasonal festivals offer unique experiences that highlight the region's agricultural bounty, history, and artisanal culture.

Autumn: Celebrating the Harvest and Local Bounty

Autumn in Dordogne is a time for harvesting the region's rich produce and showcasing the culinary traditions that make the area a foodie's paradise. As the vineyards and orchards yield their fruits, the local festivals provide a perfect opportunity to taste the fruits of the season.

- **Fête de la Noix (Walnut Festival)**

The Fête de la Noix is one of Dordogne's most beloved autumn festivals, dedicated to celebrating the region's famous walnut harvest. Walnuts have been a staple of Dordogne's agricultural economy for centuries, and this festival, typically held in the village of Creysse in October, is a delightful way to explore the region's rich connection to this harvest. Visitors can sample a wide variety of walnut-based products, from fresh nuts and walnut oil to pastries and savory dishes. The market stalls are filled with local artisans selling walnut woodcrafts, jewelry, and other walnut-inspired items. Live music, traditional dances, and family-friendly activities add to the festive atmosphere, making it a perfect event for all ages.

In addition to the walnut festivities, visitors will find regional specialties on offer, such as walnut cake, walnut jam, and walnut liqueur, making it a delicious celebration of local produce. The Fête de la Noix is also an excellent opportunity to discover Dordogne's charming countryside and enjoy the beautiful autumn colors of its forests and fields.

Winter: Embracing the Holiday Spirit and Cozy Traditions

Winter in Dordogne may be quieter than the bustling summer months, but the region's Christmas markets and festive activities ensure that there's no shortage of holiday cheer. Villages and towns across Dordogne transform into cozy, twinkling winter wonderlands, offering visitors a chance to enjoy the warmth and charm of the region during the festive season.

• Christmas Markets

Dordogne's Christmas markets are a magical experience, with the historic towns of Sarlat, Bergerac, and Périgueux hosting some of the most enchanting celebrations. These markets typically open in early December and run through the Christmas season, providing a wonderful way to get into the holiday spirit. The market in Sarlat, one of the most popular in the region, is particularly stunning. The medieval streets are illuminated with festive lights, and the air is filled with the scent of mulled wine, roasted chestnuts, and fresh pastries.

Local artisans offer a range of handcrafted goods, including pottery, jewelry, wooden toys, and intricate decorations, perfect for finding unique gifts. Vendors also sell traditional Dordogne treats like foie gras, truffles, and local cheeses, allowing visitors to sample the best of the region's holiday fare. The atmosphere is both festive and intimate, offering a chance to connect with locals, experience the warmth of their hospitality, and enjoy the slower pace of life in the winter months.

In addition to Sarlat, the Bergerac Christmas Market is known for its charming layout along the town's medieval streets, with stalls offering everything from artisanal candles to traditional wooden toys. Périgueux also hosts a beautifully decorated market with a wide array of festive foods, handcrafted gifts, and traditional French holiday items. For those looking for a more intimate experience, many of the smaller towns and villages in Dordogne also host smaller Christmas markets, each with its own unique character and charm.

- **New Year's Celebrations**

While Dordogne is known for its quieter pace during the winter months, New Year's Eve offers a festive conclusion to the year. Many restaurants and inns across the region offer special New Year's Eve dinners, often featuring a multi-course meal with local specialties like foie gras, duck confit, and truffle dishes. For a more public celebration, towns like Sarlat host lively parties with music and fireworks, while others gather for intimate celebrations in the town squares. It's a perfect way to toast the New Year in one of France's most scenic and historic regions.

Why Dordogne's Autumn and Winter Festivals Are So Special

What sets Dordogne's autumn and winter festivals apart is their ability to combine the region's deep-rooted agricultural heritage with the warmth and joy of the holiday season. In autumn, the harvest festivals like the Fête de la Noix provide an opportunity to celebrate the fruits of the land, while in winter, the Christmas markets create a magical atmosphere where locals and visitors alike come together to celebrate the season's traditions.

These festivals allow you to experience the authentic charm of Dordogne, a region where food, tradition, and community are at the heart of every celebration. Whether you're sampling local walnuts and regional delicacies or exploring the twinkling Christmas lights in a medieval village, Dordogne's seasonal festivals offer a rich, immersive experience that will leave you with lasting memories of this enchanting region.

CHAPTER 8: PRACTICAL INFORMATION FOR YOUR TRIP TO DORDOGNE

When planning your trip to Dordogne, it's important to be prepared for the region's specific health and safety conditions, weather patterns, local etiquette, and travel logistics. Understanding these aspects will ensure that your experience is not only enjoyable but also smooth and stress-free.

Health & Safety in Dordogne

Dordogne is a relatively safe and welcoming region, with well-maintained infrastructure and medical facilities, though there are some considerations to keep in mind.

- **Basic Medical Information**

Dordogne has a range of medical services available, including general practitioners, pharmacies, and hospitals. The largest medical centers are found in towns like Périgueux and Bergerac. Smaller towns and villages may have medical practices or pharmacies for basic needs. It is always a good idea to have travel health insurance that covers medical expenses, especially if you're planning on engaging in outdoor activities like hiking or canoeing, which come with their own risks.

In case of medical emergencies, you can call 112 (the European Union emergency number) for police, fire, or ambulance services. For non-urgent medical needs, you can contact local pharmacies or a doctor's office. Pharmacies in Dordogne often have extended hours, especially in tourist areas, and most pharmacists speak basic English.

- **Emergency Contacts**

- Emergency Services (Police, Fire, Ambulance): 112 (EU emergency number)

- Local Hospital in Périgueux: CHR de Périgueux – 05 53 53 80 00

• Local Hospital in Bergerac: Centre Hospitalier de Bergerac – 05 53 63 63 63

• Pharmacy: Pharmacies are widely available in both rural and urban areas. For urgent needs, consult the nearest pharmacy. Pharmacies also often have an emergency number posted outside.

• **Travel Insurance**

Travel insurance is essential when traveling in Dordogne, particularly if you're planning outdoor adventures such as hiking in the Périgord Noir, canoeing down the Dordogne River, or exploring caves. It's wise to ensure your travel insurance covers medical care, accidents, trip cancellations, and any activities you plan to participate in.

Weather in Dordogne

Dordogne is known for its relatively mild climate, but understanding the region's seasonal weather patterns can help you pack appropriately and plan your activities.

• **Summer (June - August):**

Summer in Dordogne can be hot, with temperatures regularly reaching 30°C (86°F) or higher, particularly in July and August. The warm temperatures make it a perfect time for outdoor activities such as hiking, kayaking, and exploring the region's picturesque villages and castles. However, the heat can be intense, especially in the south of the region, so it's important to stay hydrated and wear sunscreen. Evenings can be cooler, with temperatures dropping to around 15°C (59°F), so it's advisable to bring a light jacket or sweater.

- **Autumn (September - November):**

Autumn in Dordogne is a beautiful time to visit, with the foliage turning vibrant shades of red, orange, and gold. The temperatures begin to cool down, averaging around 15°C (59°F) during the day and 5-10°C (41-50°F) in the evenings. While the weather is typically mild, you should expect some rain, particularly in October and November. It's a great time to visit the region for harvest festivals, wine tasting, and scenic walks in the countryside.

- **Winter (December - February):**

Winter in Dordogne is generally cool, with daytime temperatures ranging from 5°C to 10°C (41°F to 50°F). However, freezing temperatures and snow are rare in this part of France, making it a mild winter destination. Although the weather may be chilly, winter also offers fewer tourists, and many villages are beautifully decorated for the Christmas season. If you plan on visiting during this time, be prepared for some rain, and pack warm clothing and layers.

- **Spring (March - May):**

Spring in Dordogne brings milder temperatures and blossoming flowers, making it a lovely time to visit. Average temperatures range from 10°C to 18°C (50°F to 64°F), with the weather gradually warming as the season progresses. Rain is more frequent in the spring months, so it's a good idea to bring a waterproof jacket and an umbrella.

Local Etiquette

Dordogne is a region known for its friendly and welcoming locals, but like many parts of France, there are some cultural norms that visitors should be aware of to ensure they are respectful and well-received.

- **Greetings**

In rural areas like Dordogne, it's customary to greet locals with a simple "Bonjour" (good day) when entering shops, restaurants, or small villages. While many people in tourist areas will speak English, using a basic French greeting is appreciated and shows respect for local culture. In smaller towns, it's especially important to be polite and make an effort to learn a few basic phrases in French.

- Tipping

In France, tipping is not obligatory, but it is appreciated for good service. In restaurants, a service charge is usually included in the bill (indicated by "service compris"), but if you've had particularly excellent service, it's common to leave a small tip (5-10% of the bill). For taxi drivers or hotel staff, rounding up the fare or leaving a couple of extra euros is a nice gesture.

- **Dress Code**

French people tend to dress neatly and stylishly, even in casual settings. While there is no strict dress code for tourists, it's recommended to avoid overly casual clothing such as shorts and flip-flops when visiting restaurants or cultural sites. In churches or during religious ceremonies, modest dress is expected.

- **Respecting Traditions**

In small towns and villages, be mindful of local customs. For example, be quiet and respectful in the morning when locals are heading to church or starting their day. It's also customary to avoid disturbing others during mealtimes, particularly in rural areas where family meals are an important part of daily life.

Key Travel Tips for Dordogne

- Language: While French is the official language in Dordogne, many people in tourist areas will speak some English. However, learning a few basic French phrases (such as "Bonjour" for good day, "Merci" for thank you, and "Excusez-moi" for excuse me) will go a long way in making connections with locals and showing respect for their culture.

- Electrical Outlets: France uses the standard Type C and Type E power outlets, so make sure to bring the appropriate adapter and converter if needed.

- Cash vs. Credit: While most places accept credit cards, small shops, cafés, and rural markets may prefer cash, particularly in more remote villages. It's always a good idea to carry some cash, especially if you plan on visiting smaller, more traditional areas. ATMs are widely available in towns like Sarlat, Périgueux, and Bergerac.

By keeping these practical considerations in mind, you'll be fully equipped to have a safe, enjoyable, and respectful visit to Dordogne, allowing you to immerse yourself in the region's natural beauty, history, and unique cultural experiences.

CHAPTER 9: SAMPLE ITINERARIES FOR DORDOGNE

Dordogne offers a variety of experiences, from exploring its medieval towns to hiking through lush valleys and enjoying world-class cuisine. Whether you have just a few days or a full week, there are itineraries that will allow you to get the most out of this enchanting region. Here are two sample itineraries for different types of travelers: a quick 3-day highlights tour and a more immersive 5-day experience.

3-Day Highlights Tour: Explore Iconic Medieval Towns, Castles, and Prehistoric Caves

Day 1: Medieval Towns and Dordogne River Views

- **Morning:**

Arrive in Sarlat-la-Canéda, one of the most well-preserved medieval towns in France. Wander through its cobbled streets, lined with stone buildings, and explore the Place de la Liberté, the central square where you can enjoy the vibrant market (if it's market day). Take time to appreciate the beautiful architecture, especially the grand Saint-Sacerdos Cathedral.

- **Lunch:**

Enjoy a traditional meal at a local bistro, perhaps sampling the famous foie gras or a hearty French cassoulet.

- **Afternoon:**

After lunch, drive or take a short trip to La Roque-Gageac, a picturesque village perched against a cliff along the Dordogne River. The views here are stunning, and you can visit the troglodyte dwellings, caves carved into the rock. For a truly unique experience, consider taking a gabarre boat tour along the river, which will give you beautiful views of the village and surrounding landscape.

- **Evening:**

Return to Sarlat for dinner at a traditional French restaurant. Try the local truffle dishes if you're visiting in the fall, as the region is renowned for its truffles.

Day 2: Castles, History, and Culinary Delights

• **Morning:**

Start your day with a visit to Château de Beynac, one of the most striking castles in Dordogne, offering magnificent views over the Dordogne River. Take a guided tour to learn about its fascinating medieval history. Afterward, drive to Château de Castelnaud, a medieval fortress offering interactive exhibits on medieval warfare.

• **Lunch:**

Head to the nearby village of Beynac-et-Cazenac for lunch at a local café. Enjoy regional specialties like confit de canard or duck pâté en croûte.

• **Afternoon:**

In the afternoon, visit the world-famous Lascaux Caves to witness the awe-inspiring prehistoric cave art. The original caves are closed to the public to preserve the artwork, but the Lascaux IV replica provides an excellent immersive experience. Spend the rest of the afternoon at Les Eyzies-de-Tayac-Sireuil, the prehistory capital of the world, and explore its many museums dedicated to early human history.

• **Evening:**

Return to Sarlat or another nearby town and enjoy dinner at a local restaurant. Try a regional wine, such as Bergerac, paired with local cheese.

Day 3: Outdoor Adventure and Local Markets

- **Morning:**

On your final day, head to the Vézère Valley, a UNESCO World Heritage site known for its prehistoric sites and beautiful scenery. Take a hike through this stunning landscape, or if you're feeling adventurous, try canoeing or kayaking on the Vézère River.

- **Lunch:**

Stop in a charming village like Domme for a light lunch. The medieval town offers stunning views over the Dordogne Valley, and you can explore its cliffside streets and fortress.

- **Afternoon:**

Visit the local Sarlat Market if it's market day, or explore other nearby towns like Bergerac, known for its wine and historic center. Explore the Place Pelissière, the heart of Bergerac, with its quaint streets and picturesque architecture.

- **Evening:**

Finish your day with a final dinner in one of Dordogne's top restaurants. Savor a meal that includes tarte aux noix (walnut tart) or another dessert made from local produce.

5-Day Immersion: Outdoor Activities, Historical Sites, and Culinary Experiences

Day 1: Arrival and Medieval Towns

- ### Morning:

Arrive in Sarlat and begin your exploration of this beautiful medieval town. Wander through its maze of streets, stopping at Place de la Liberté, and visit the Saint-Sacerdos Cathedral. Don't miss a visit to the Maison de la Boétie, the house of the famous philosopher Étienne de La Boétie.

- ### Lunch:

Enjoy a leisurely lunch at a local café, trying regional delicacies such as goat cheese or foie gras.

- ### Afternoon:

After lunch, drive to La Roque-Gageac for a boat tour along the Dordogne River. Explore the village's troglodyte caves and take in the spectacular cliffs.

- ### Evening:

Dine in Sarlat, where you can find a selection of French restaurants offering everything from simple bistro meals to more sophisticated dishes.

Day 2: Châteaux, Wine Tasting, and Culinary Delights

- **Morning:**

Drive to Château de Castelnaud and Château de Beynac, two of Dordogne's most stunning castles. Explore the medieval architecture, walk around the ramparts, and visit the on-site museums.

- **Lunch:**

Enjoy a wine-tasting lunch in the Bergerac wine region, famous for its Monbazillac wines. Take a vineyard tour and sample local wines paired with gourmet French food.

- **Afternoon:**

Visit Château des Milandes, the former home of Josephine Baker, for a look into the life of the famous American dancer. The château's beautiful gardens are perfect for a relaxed stroll.

- **Evening:**

Head to Bergerac for dinner at a local restaurant. Try a regional dish such as duck confit or truffle-based cuisine, and pair it with a glass of Bergerac wine.

Day 3: Prehistoric Sites and Outdoor Adventures

- **Morning:**

Visit Lascaux IV, a replica of the famous Lascaux Caves, to see some of the world's most famous prehistoric cave art. Afterwards, head to Les Eyzies-de-Tayac-Sireuil and explore the many archaeological sites.

- **Lunch:**

Stop for lunch in a nearby village like Montignac, enjoying local specialties like walnut salad or pâté de foie gras.

- **Afternoon:**

Spend the afternoon exploring the Vézère Valley. If you're feeling adventurous, go canoeing or kayaking down the river, or take a walk through the valley to visit some of the prehistoric caves.

- **Evening:**

Return to Sarlat for a delicious dinner. Try regional specialties such as duck pâté en croûte or a hearty cassoulet.

Day 4: Scenic Villages and Hiking

- **Morning:**

Spend the day hiking in the Perigord Noir, an area of dense forests, rivers, and picturesque villages. Start in Domme, a medieval bastide town, where you can enjoy breathtaking views over the Dordogne River.

- **Lunch:**

Pack a picnic lunch or stop in one of the quaint villages along the way for a local meal. Try truffle-based dishes or simple French country fare.

- **Afternoon:**

Continue your hike through the region's lush countryside, visiting charming villages such as Beynac-et-Cazenac and Castelnaud-la-Chapelle.

- **Evening:**

End your day at a traditional French restaurant, where you can enjoy a hearty meal of duck confit, foie gras, and truffle-based dishes.

Day 5: Relaxation and Market Visits

- **Morning:**

On your final day, explore the local Sarlat Market, one of the best markets in France, offering everything from fresh produce to artisanal goods. It's a great place to buy regional products like truffles, walnuts, and cheese.

- **Lunch:**

Enjoy a leisurely lunch in Sarlat, savoring local specialties or simply a classic French meal.

- **Afternoon:**

If you have time before departure, visit the Dordogne River for a peaceful boat tour or a final visit to one of the charming local towns.

- **Evening:**

Wrap up your Dordogne experience with a relaxed dinner in one of the village's best eateries. Enjoy a tarte aux noix (walnut tart) for dessert before heading back.

Whether you opt for a whirlwind 3-day tour or a deeper 5-day immersion, Dordogne will provide an unforgettable blend of history, nature, and gastronomy. Each day brings new experiences, from the breathtaking medieval architecture to the scenic beauty of the rivers and caves, ensuring that your time in this enchanting region is filled with discovery and delight.

Family-Friendly Itinerary: Kid-Friendly Castles, Outdoor Adventures, and Easy Hikes in Dordogne

Dordogne is a wonderful destination for families looking for an enriching yet relaxing vacation. With its fairytale-like castles, gentle rivers, and safe, scenic trails, the region offers a perfect mix of outdoor adventure, culture, and hands-on activities for children of all ages. Here's a 5-day family-friendly itinerary that will keep everyone entertained and engaged, while offering a great balance of fun and relaxation.

Day 1: Arrival and Exploration of Sarlat

• Morning:

Arrive in Sarlat-la-Canéda, a beautiful medieval town known for its charming streets and laid-back atmosphere. The town is very walkable, making it perfect for families with children. Begin with a relaxed stroll through the cobblestone streets, stopping to admire the medieval architecture. Kids will love the narrow alleys, fountains, and historic buildings.

- Lunch:

Stop for lunch at a family-friendly café. Opt for simple dishes like crepes, quiches, or croque-monsieur, which are sure to please even the pickiest eaters.

- Afternoon:

In the afternoon, head to the Sarlat Market if it's market day. It's a lively and colorful place, where children can explore local produce, cheeses, and other regional goods. You can also pick up some snacks or souvenirs to take home. Afterward, take a gentle walk to Place de la Liberté, the central square where the whole family can relax.

- Evening:

Finish the day with a casual dinner at one of Sarlat's family-friendly restaurants. Many offer a "menu enfant" (children's menu), which often includes French favorites like steak frites or grilled chicken.

Day 2: Castles and Medieval Adventures

- Morning:

Start your day by visiting Château de Beynac, one of Dordogne's most iconic castles. Set on a cliff with dramatic views over the Dordogne River, this castle is not only an amazing historical site but also a fun experience for kids. The castle has a large courtyard, ramparts to walk on, and plenty of space for children to run around. The castle is also interactive, with guided tours that bring the medieval period to life.

- Lunch:

Head to the nearby village of Beynac-et-Cazenac for lunch. Choose a cozy, family-friendly restaurant where you can enjoy local specialties like duck confit or simpler French dishes like omelettes.

- Afternoon:

In the afternoon, visit Château de Castelnaud, another stunning fortress with a focus on medieval warfare. This interactive museum has lots of hands-on exhibits that kids will love, including armor displays and a large collection of medieval weapons. The castle's grounds also provide a great opportunity for children to explore.

- Evening:

Return to Sarlat for dinner, perhaps trying a family-style fondue or another classic French dish that can be shared.

Day 3: Prehistoric Sites and Outdoor Adventures

- Morning:

Spend the morning exploring Les Eyzies-de-Tayac-Sireuil, the prehistory capital of the world. Start with a visit to the Prehistory Museum, which is both educational and interactive for children. The museum has models of prehistoric animals, life-size reconstructions of early human dwellings, and exhibits on cave art that kids will find fascinating.

- Lunch:

Head to a nearby café in Les Eyzies or a small village along the way for a casual lunch. Enjoy some hearty French classics like croissants, soupe à l'oignon (onion soup), or cheese platters.

- Afternoon:

In the afternoon, take a family-friendly hike in the Vézère Valley, a UNESCO World Heritage site known for its prehistoric caves and natural beauty. The trails here are easy and suitable for children, offering an opportunity to enjoy both nature and history. For an even more hands-on experience, you can visit Font-de-Gaume, one of the last caves with prehistoric paintings still open to the public.

- Evening:

Return to Sarlat for a relaxing dinner and perhaps a walk around the town square to wind down the day.

Day 4: Canoeing and Village Exploration

- Morning:

Start the day with a family-friendly canoeing trip along the Dordogne River. There are plenty of rental companies offering guided canoe tours suitable for families, with no prior experience required. Paddle down the calm river, taking in the stunning views of castles, cliffs, and lush greenery. This is a perfect way to enjoy the outdoors while keeping kids engaged.

- Lunch:

Stop at a riverside café for a simple lunch. Many places along the river offer casual dining with outdoor seating, where kids can enjoy the open space while parents relax.

- Afternoon:

After lunch, visit La Roque-Gageac, one of the most beautiful villages in France. The village is located along the river, with its traditional stone houses and cliffside views. Take a gentle walk through the village, stopping to explore the troglodyte dwellings and the beautiful gardens at Jardins de Marqueyssac. The garden has a hedge maze that children will enjoy navigating.

- Evening:

Dinner in La Roque-Gageac or return to Sarlat. Many restaurants in the region offer family-friendly options like grilled fish, charcuterie platters, or kid's portions of regional specialties.

Day 5: Fun and Relaxation

- Morning:

For a more relaxed day, take a trip to the Dordogne River, where you can enjoy some beach time or a casual walk along the riverbanks. Kids can paddle, skip stones, or simply relax in the calm waters. Alternatively, you could visit Dordogne's parks and gardens, such as the Jardins de l'Imaginaire in Terrasson-Lavilledieu, where there are playful sculptures, fountains, and plenty of open space for children to run around.

- Lunch:

Have a laid-back lunch at a riverside café or picnic in one of the parks. Choose simple and child-friendly food such as sandwiches, fruit, or ice cream.

- Afternoon:

In the afternoon, visit Domme, a charming medieval bastide town that's easy to explore with children. Take the kids to the Cave of Domme, an underground passageway where they can learn about the town's history. The village's main square is perfect for some relaxing downtime with ice cream.

- Evening:

For your final dinner in Dordogne, indulge in a shared family meal featuring tarte aux noix (walnut tart) or crepes for dessert.

Additional Tips for Families:

- Interactive Experiences: Many of Dordogne's sites offer child-friendly activities, from medieval workshops at castles to hands-on exhibits at museums.

- Local Markets: Exploring a local market is a great way to introduce kids to French food and culture. They can pick out their own snacks or souvenirs.

- Kid-Friendly Accommodation: Look for hotels, gîtes, or vacation rentals with family-friendly amenities like swimming pools or large gardens. Many accommodations in Dordogne cater specifically to families.

•   Pace Yourself: Make sure to balance activity-filled days with slower-paced mornings or afternoons to avoid overwhelming the children, especially during the summer heat.

This family-friendly itinerary in Dordogne is perfect for those who want to blend outdoor fun, history, and local culture while making lasting memories with children. From medieval castles to river adventures, every moment is packed with discovery and joy for the whole family.

CHAPTER 10: FINAL WORDS

Dordogne is a destination that transcends time, where every corner offers an opportunity for discovery. From its meandering rivers perfect for paddling to its medieval villages steeped in history, the region is a treasure trove of experiences waiting to be explored. Whether you're wandering through cobblestone streets, savoring a meal of foie gras and truffles, or simply soaking in the stunning natural beauty, the allure of Dordogne lies in its ability to slow you down and draw you in.

This is a place where life moves at a gentler pace, offering the chance to truly connect with the land, its people, and its rich heritage. Whether you're a history buff, a nature enthusiast, or a food lover, Dordogne delivers an experience that lingers long after you've left. Take your time, savor each moment, and let the tranquility and charm of this remarkable region captivate your heart, just as it has done for generations of travelers.

GET ACCESS TO MORE BOOKS BY THE AUTHOR

Printed in Great Britain
by Amazon

62112937R00090